Puptent Poets

Puptent Poets

Of the
Stars and Stripes
Mediterranean

Compiled by
CPL. Charles A. Hogan & CPL. John Welsh, III

Illustrated by
SGT. Stanley Meltzoff

Edited by
LT. Ed Hill

Washington, D.C.

© Ross & Perry, Inc. 2002 on new material. All rights reserved.

No claim to U.S. government work contained throughout this book.

Protected under the Berne Convention.

Printed in The United States of America
Ross & Perry, Inc. Publishers
216 G St., N.E.,
Washington, D.C. 20002
Telephone (202) 675-8300
Facsimile (801)459-7535
info@RossPerry.com

SAN 253-8555

Government Reprints Press Edition 2002

Government Reprints Press is an Imprint of Ross & Perry, Inc.

Library of Congress Control Number: 2001095411
http://www.GPOreprints.com

ISBN 1-931641-98-6

Book Cover designed by Sapna/sapna@rossperry.com

♾ The paper used in this publication meets the requirements for permanence established by the American National Standard for Information Sciences "Permanence of Paper for Printed Library Materials" (ANSI Z39.48-1984).

All rights reserved. No copyrighted part of this publication may be reproduced, stored in a retrieval system, or transmitted, in any form or by any means, electronic, photocopying, recording, or otherwise, without the prior written permission of the publisher.

Foreword

Throughout the Mediterranean Theater of war, it is respectable to be a poet.

Men in uniform who might once have regarded poetry as a matter for "long hairs" and "softies," are writing poems themselves and, what's more, signing them.

Truck drivers are no less inclined toward the muse than the company cook; a machinegunner will dash off a verse during the lull of battle; the stony-faced topkick is producing love lyrics, and there's a laureate in every company. As one CO remarked:

"It's a wonder we get any work done."

The birth of the Puptent Poet took place more than two years ago when The Stars and Stripes, Mediterranean, in its first issue published in Algiers, opened its columns to soldier verse.

It was a modest beginning. A mail censor named Lt. Gillespie turned in a few stanzas on the theme that he had accidentally slashed up one of his own letters while censoring company mail. The next issue contained a cynical, anonymous verse berating the thick mud of Oran.

It may not have been apparent at the time, but the two versifiers had set a pattern for two years of Mediterranean poetry. From the beginning, the poetry department of The Stars and Stripes was open to all ranks. Furthermore, no one had to be a great poet, nor even a very good one to break into print.

Poems came in faster than the editors had dared to hope. From Casablanca to the sand-swept wadis of Tunisia, soldiers struck out boldly, discovering first that some things were better said in poetry than prose and, second, that The Stars and Stripes would publish what they wrote.

Critical standards set by newspapers in the United States were never adopted. Poetry critics were not allowed on the premises. What went into the paper was the best of the Army's verse-making that day, or that week. If the meter was wobbly and the rhymes eccentric or missing, no one got excited.

In two years of Puptent Poetry, no great war poet has revealed himself. What the Puptent Poets department has provided is a kind of open forum whose only requirements are a poetic leaning and an interest in writing about the war as well as living it. The result has been about 1,000 published poems in a little more than two years, and about 15 times that figure filed or returned to the writer with a note of regret.

Returning these notes and encouraging the Puptent Poets to try again has given Cpl. John Welsh, III, of Washington, D. C., a steady job as chief poetry editor and has made him one of the busiest correspondents in the theater.

Together with Cpl. Charles A. Hogan, of Trenton, N. J., who served as poetry editor of the Naples edition before going to France in a similar capacity, Cpl. Welsh compiled this the first Stars and Stripes Puptent Poet anthology.

—*The Editors.*

HATRED'S YIELD

I've seen "the crosses row on row,"
I've seen the graves at Anzio.
In Flanders fields men cannot sleep—
Their faith, the world found hard to keep.
Versailles' fate was slyly sealed
Before earth's gaping wounds had healed,
And now again rows of crosses
Mutely tell of nations' losses.
In how many fields,
In how many lands
Will soldiers die by soldiers' hands?
Until at long last mankind yields
To truth and reason's studied choice
Ignoring hatred's strident voice.

—Pvt. Jack P. Nantell

FIELD MOVIE

Beneath a starry summer sky,
Upon a stubbled field,
The soldiers sprawl enraptured
While a movie is unreeled.
They weep and laugh with shadows,
They gasp at acted strife,
Drink deep of formula romance
Embrace a synthetic life,
But these soldiers move in pageant
More vast than any seen,
And know it not—for them
Drama lives upon a screen.

—Sgt. Virgil Scott

TEMPUS FUGIT

While Riding a 40 and 8 in North Africa

This land which once was strewn with blood,
Symbol of mighty clannish passions—
Now is littered with GI mud
And used up tins of old C-rations.

—W-O (j.g.) Henry J. Foner

HANDS

I lay there
And all I could see and feel
Were her hands.
Hands . . .
White, clean and kind,
Impersonal
But ministering to my wants
Talking to me
Telling me again
That there was goodness in life
That would bring me
Green valleys in springtime
These hands could brush a fevered brow
And make it cool again
As morning air . . .
The first day of April.

—Pfc. Harry Olive

HEY BUD

Hey Bud,
Watch out, will ya! This one's close!
Whoops! Whatta splash! That's a dud!
Where in the hell . . . ya goin'?

Hey Bud,
Stop, will ya? Ain'cha scared?
Looka that grass red with blood!
Why d'ya keep on goin'?
Ya don't wanna kill do ya?
But ya gonna kill, by God
Ya gotta get goin'.

Hey Bud,
Ya tired? Wanna go ta bed?
Don't go ta sleep in that mud!
—Oh—gotta a hole—in—ya—head
Sorry—Bud—
I'll—I'll keep on goin'.
      —Sgt. Masque

ORDER

"At eight AM we're pulling out,"
The general sternly said,
So the colonel sent the order down,
"At five we leave our bed."
Well, the captain took no chances,
Because captains never do,
And so he told the topkick,
"Have the men get up at two."
At midnight the sergeant woke us,
And here we sadly sit,
Because it now is noontime,
And we haven't pulled out yet.
   —T-5 Carl D. Westerberg

DIRTY GERTIE *

Dirty Gertie from Bizerte
Hid a mousetrap 'neath her skertie,
Strapped it on her kneecap purty,
Baited it with Fleur de Flirte,
Made her boy friends most alerty,
She was voted in Bizerte
"Miss Latrine" for nineteen-thirty.
—Pvt. William L. Russell

FANNY OF TRAPANI

Rumor has it "Dirty Gertie,"
Whom you knew in old Bizerte,
Has a sister in Trapani
By the name of Filthy Fanny.
She is Gertie's black-sheep sister,
No man yet has ever kissed her,
Though her friends have never told her
Awful is her body odor.
What a frightful-looking creature!
Badly formed in every feature!
When she ran for "MISS LATRINE"
The judges cried for Atabrine.
Fellows, now that you're in Trapani,
Be on the watch for "Filthy Fanny."
—Cpl. F. D. Conner

*The original version of "Dirty Gertie," published in YANK, differed slightly from the verse reprinted in The Stars and Stripes. While "Gertie" was not a protege of "Puptent Poets," the editors felt nonetheless that she should be included in any collection of "the girls" discovered by Mediterranean military meanderers.

LUSCIOUS LENA

Luscious Lena from Messina,
Cutest thing you've ever seena;
All the GI's dream—a queena!
Oh, that skin of sultry sheena!
When you go into Messina,
She will drink from your canteena;
She won't sock you on the beana,
But will purr like a machina.
When you walk through fields so greena,
With this lovely, luscious Lena;
She will say: "No go—bambina . . ."
(Hard to keep this ending cleena).

—Cpl. Fred Fischer
Pfc. Floyd Allchin

MARIE OF NAPOLI

My fair Marie of Napoli
Has taste and more
Her figure's round,
A perfect thirty-four.
Her build is slight,
Her step is light,
Her lips are sweet as dew.
Her cheek so fair, her silken hair,
Her eyes of gold-flecked brown;
The merest touch, and you want to clutch
The neatest stuff in town.
But halt your glim, for your chance is slim,
Forget your dearest wish,
It's tough stuff, lad, and just too bad
But you see, I found her first!

—Pvt. James F. Dunne

MY NAME IS TINA

(All names are fictitious)

My name is Tina and I love the Allies; my home
Is in Pagliano, Ravello, in Campania.
I was born there in spring, I live there still,
With my mother and my sister, God willing,
We shall die in peace there.

Before the war, I was happy as I worked in the fields
For my father who had land around San Mertino.
One day, he was too near the fighting men,
And, deserted by God, did not return—
His body, or a piece, lies there . . .

There where his sweat had dripped into the soil
Where his long labors had been so freely expended,
He stretched stiff and still with a smile
On his grey face; and we all wept as women weep.
And the soft wind was a sigh there.

Then the Allies came to the village school, only a few.
Some were quiet, kind, but aloof.
One, a fair captain called Hirsh:
He was kindly, but, too, stood aloof
From my family, yet, would speak of Boston
And home and some sort of tie there.
With my officer came other Americans, lean,
Good-looking men, laughing and never aloof
And I loved one called Bankes (I think)—
He said: "Wherever you are, Honey child—
My poor dog-gone heart will fly there."

Yes, that's what he said. He loved me and loved me well.
His child is in my womb and I, lonely fool,
I cry for the moon, I cry as if I had
Shed no tears before; I bury my face in the bed
There where we slept—thus I cry there.

My name is Tina, and I love the Allies.
Magnani, the doctor in our village, wants his money before
He will help me. Captain Hirsh understands.
Captain Hirsh left today—but he paid Magnani,
I love Boston. I too, have a tie there — —

—Capt. Frederick Brundle

CROSSING

(From the pages of a GI's Diary)

Through the white danger of the crowded waves
A convoy plows within its iron lines.
One soldier wonders how much love she saves
For him back home; another squints for signs
Of land; another throws his dinner up;
Another reads "Ten Murdered," at the rail;
Another dreams of coffee in a cup
With cream and sugar and a buttered snail;
A few have pocketed the Testament
The smiling Chaplains pressed into their hands
As they shot craps with marvelous content.
One fat dark boy is careful where he stands:
No one can see the tears form in his eyes—
The ships continue while his father dies.

—Sgt. Ray Reynolds

MADNESS

If war be madness learn from it my friend
That two and two do not always make four,
Night may not follow day, nor slaves adore
The master's brazen bounty to the end.

There's pain in beauty, for the two must blend,
To flower harmoniously, and there is more
Hideousness than truth in all the lore
Of science reeking with the deceptive trend.

Before you pay the debt you owe for living,
Choose well t'wixt art and sense, wisdom and knowledge.
What havoc has man wrought, what silly madness!
Drink in the power your heart is giving
And scotch his logic, redolent of college
Stand alone, or cringe if this be madness.

—Lt. Lester Weil

EL GUETTAR

And so we meet again at El Guettar.
From Thala where we sent you reeling back;
Now once again you'll feel our furious might
And shrink before the steel of our attack.
For wrongs still unavenged and rights denied
A bloody reckoning be yours to know;
You'll curse the dawn and dread the darkening night,
And fear shall make the very winds be foe.

—Pvt. R. R. Newcomb

DJEBEL AKROUTA

Faid Pass, '43

The starlit night closed in
On land that day which felt
Heavy cannonading ... screams of men
In the shadow of mosques and minarets.
A falling star shot across the silvered
Night, a long, long moment it curved
And faded on a treeless hill—dead,
Its glorious moment done on earth.
The dark had closed once more, all still.
God, what shapeless form is on that hill?
A beast at sleep? A man at rest? A shrub?
What could sleep, or rest, or grow
On top that barren rise so sheer, so cold:
Lord, a man! A lad with scant beard!
See, in his hand a gun ... on his breast, red;
His glorious moment done on earth,
No uniform is his—what matters now ...
His lips may have spoke of town or plow—
His nose could have sniffed the Georgian pine—
His eyes, perchance, had seen the twisting Rhine—
But, he lay shot: fair game in the hunt, the war.
God, when it is at end, will there be more?
Will leaders of the crowd find reason
To open, man against man, another season ...

—Pvt. Ray Wheaton

IN CONSTANTINE

Remember how we stood on a cliff
And watched the city in its Sunday mood?
A city on a mountain top, like a dream
Fashioned in stone, surrounded
By the Rhumel in all its
Tremendous glory . . .
Remember how we watched a playful hawk
Soar on the wind currents—dive and dip,
Careen . . . and fly away into the sun,
Only to return again and again
Sailing gracefully as a swan
Upon a mirror lake . . .
I studied your face. The evening sun
Danced in your eyes, the wild wind blowing
Through your hair, a happy face
Above the world of reality.
I loved your laughter. Like the hawk,
It too soared heavenward on the winds
Of the Rhumel; high into the sky
Only to be lost in space.
—Pvt. M. A. Decker-Boyle

POTENT ABDULLAH

On the sands of North Morocco
Stood a tent, complete with Arabs
Stood the home of old Abdullah
Potent ruler of the desert;
From the goat he made him wallets,
From the tin he made him bracelets,
From the camel made he purses,
Sold them to the tough invaders . . .
From the men he bummed the bon-bon
And the chocolat, and the chew-goom,
Took them to the wife and children
To the tent, complete with Arabs
To the home of old Abdullah
Potent ruler of the desert.
—Lt. M. E. Mercer

TREMENDOUS WINGS

You came, as winter winds come,
Rushing through war's stormy skies.
You heard the beat of faroff drums
That sounds on the soul of Freedom's cries:
You felt the way all men must feel
(That reeling flash of remembering)
When pinions fail and mighty wings
Fall broken like some anguished thing
Into eternity's oblivion . . .
I pray you knew, felt, saw or heard,
In that brief time between
The men who stayed to catch your torch
With strong quick hands unseen,
You flew with ease, like winter clouds
Shadowing the scarred earth under.
Then hand in hand with immortal crowds
You heard, like a clap of thunder,
Your plane burst fire and twisted steel
Replaced the pilot's stick and wheel.
Then seeing your broken man made wings
Ablaze in a man-made hell,
I think you smiled a saddened smile
At the tiny distance you fell.
You flew with ease, like winter clouds—
Like winter winds, you stayed awhile
Then off in a rush, like the song of the thrush,
To the lovely land of spring.

—Lt. Winifred Cochran, ANC

YOU WILL BE OLD

You will be old, you will be old . . .
This is a benison, a balm
For those, like me, who must behold
Your beauty in this cruel calm,
Its iced perfection, its retreat.
Not soon, but sometime, must the mould
Revamp your freshness, weigh your feet,
And you become a story told.

—Pvt. John L. Sheehan

RIPONE DEL VAST

Where once stood a whitewashed villa
Covered over with climbing roses,
Gay with shouts of playing children,
Hope and future of the land,
Totter now in dust and ashes
Crumbling walls of stone and plaster,
In smoking piles of debris—
Here a foot, and there a hand.
Men and women of tomorrow
Lying there in dust and silence,
Who shall carry on your future?
Who shall bear your family name?
From a box among the wreckage
Safety placed there by his mother
Just before man's hell from heaven
Took her to the great unknown,
Climbs a child of two short summers,
Unperturbed by death about him:
And, though knowing not its import,
Turns to face the coming dawn.

—T-Sgt. Stanley R. Gibson

ODE OF LAMENT

God gave the pig
A mighty snout
With which to dig
And root about.
And claws like iron
He gave the mole
With which to burrow
And dig his hole.
But God forgot
In the human riggin',
To provide a tool
For foxhole diggin'.
      —Ranger Randolph Jeck

BASIC ENGLISH

Girl think me fine;
Think marriage very nice;
Want shoe, want rice;
Me say: "Ho-hum."
Me not so dumb;
Married man no play,
Single man hey-hey;
She sob, she cry,
She find other guy;
They marry, he work,
Me think him jerk.
Jap come, drop sticks,
Me go Fort Dix.
Me keep gun clean;
They have bambine.
Me scared, she earn;
Me live, me learn.
      —Pvt. Robert D. Kenyner

ENCORE

First it's a sip,
Then another nip:
Now I'm drunk . . .
Gad, manacled . . . sunk!
      —Pfc. D. James Sawyer

TO A MESSKIT

So very often do poets write
Of flowers, birds and such,
That one gets tired of seeing them
And reading them so much.
Now, I have a thing more dear to me,
Romantic and divine,
Its shining face a symbol of
That appetite of mine.
God bless each little rivet,
The knife, the fork, the spoon—
Forever may they render forth
Their sweet metallic tune.
And when these days of corn-beef hash
Are memories all aglow,
There'll be a place for it somewhere
Where all good mess-kits go.

—Lt. H. S. Davenport

UNREQUITING

She looked at me with half-closed eyes,
And laid her head upon my shoulder;
Although I am quite worldly wise,
My heart grew only colder.
I hated her and all her kind,
This exotic, evil creature;
I know I'll have no peace of mind
'Till I forget her every feature.
If my friends could see me now
They would say I was a fool
But I have grief upon my brow
I am the nursemaid to a mule.

—Cpl. E. H. Colosacco

IMPEDIMENTA

Oh, privates let us bow our heads
And pray for this our goal—
That no human mind will e'er conceive
A portable foxhole.

—Pvt. Tom Newton

ABOUT AN ABBEY

Men killed each other in tragic fray
And a House of God stood in the way:
To this place of prayer fate had brought
Hell's fury as havoc of war was wrought
In holy halls where sandaled monks had tread,
Chanting their office for living and for dead.
'Tis not for us to judge this holocaust
Of ruins, where once a Sacred Host
Veiled God from human defections such as
 these
Devil-created maelstroms of human miseries.
For record, "Satan was driven out," will suffice
And in so doing a Temple of God was sacri-
 ficed.
Men killed each other in tragic fray
Unwittingly, a House of God stood in the way.
—S-Sgt. Robert B. Burke

TO SALERNO

Down the blue sea, sea brown
Lanes, the convoy presses
In urgent majesty,
Ship after ship long gowned
In whitest phosphorescence.
In myriad panophy
Of sparkling hues;
And ever underneath
The dull insistent meter,
The deep-set stroke of power
Of pistons pregnant
With the lust of oil.
—Musn. Stanley Popperwell

ANZIO

A flare-lit night, a frosty breeze
The chequered light of moon through trees
The gelid, quiv'ring battle glow
This is Nero's Anzio.

The monster stalks; his cannon roar
Is this Dunkirk, Corregidor?
In sharp riposte our guns bark "No"
"These are the men of Anzio."

By day the wedgewood sky is bright
With vapor trails of Allied might;
By night the scudding clouds resound
With sounds of war from air and ground.

Against this mighty fist of nail
Our lines hold firm,
They shall not fail,
Thus slowly, Europe's bloodstained yoke
Is seized from puerile herrenvolk.

This inchoate beach, this spot of sand
Beyond the Paperhanger's hand
Will share in history's hallowed glow
Remember it, this Anzio.
—Lt. Richard Oulahan Jr.

NO BED OF ROSES

When I go home to the States again
And recline on a mattressed bed,
I'll put rocks in the sheets before I can sleep
And brick-bats under my head.

—T-5 Jay Gumm

AH, WILDERNESS

Vin rouge is my favorite vin
I like to drink it slow;
Because it lights my tummy with
A faint but rosy glow.
Then I fain would quaff Vermouth
After I have ate:
It fills me with a rare good cheer
And makes me scintillate.
Muscat's an aperitif
To tease your appetite:
It makes your feet feel heavy—
Your head high as a kite.

—Sgt. George McCoy

COURTSHIP IN ITALY

Circumstances change the fashions,
Flowers and music yield to C-rations.

—S-Sgt. Edward Jasowitz

LITERARY CRITICISM

There's nothing like a puptent poem
To make me writhe in pain;
It hits and splits my weary dome
And fills me with disdain.

In all my weary life,
I never read such gush and goo;
I luv you, wuv you, cherished wife,
And I luv rosies, posies, too.

Hark, the lark, and hush the thrush,
And cock-a-doodle-doo!
Hug me, mug me, dextrose mush
Glubber-gug and gluey-goo!

"I wail, I weep, I miss you so,
O read, my sorrow overbounds,
Whisper, whimper, belch and oh!
How can soldiers make such sounds!"
—T-4 N. N. Levy

BATTLE

The blackness was in me,
Such fate and fury as I had never known:
Complete amnesia from love and spring,
And tenderness of home.
Surging through me, I could feel it rise
And lift me with it.
I was free, to lust for blood,
And I could use my hands
To tear and smash ...
My eyes to sight for killing!
The noises, whistling, wooming
In the blackness
Became a part of me,
Spurred my passion, lashed me on,
Became fused with my mind's unwholesomeness:
I would caress, with savagery,
And put them all in hell forever.
I willed to butcher as they had butchered,
Destroy as they destroyed.
I sobbed aloud as no man has ever cried:
Someone screamed, maybe me. I could smell
Powder, burnt flesh, maybe mine ...
I think I died then.
I don't want to remember any more ...
God knows—I wish I could forget.

—Sgt. S. Colker

WITH UNDYING LOVE

—And when the long siege is done,
And they set us to rest at last,
Only the knowledge that I have made you glad
Will I take with me.
Where that lies will grow a greener grass,
A greener tree.
And in that shade you will pass
Forever before my eyes,
A greater gift than all God's Paradise.

—Cpl. J. D. Countess

AIR RAID

The searchlights probe the startled night
And pin the bombers like string-held kites,
On beamed untwinkling stars of white.
The AA guns shout parrying fight,
And defy in a chorus of stammering might;
Their darting fingers are seeking bright
A pattern of deadly streaks of spite.
The bombs strike down, far left, far right
And mushrooming rumbled blights
Of noise respond . . . a hit ignites
And the fire tongues up to dizzy heights,
A broken bomber falls in tight
Plunging arcs, out, out of sight;
Then suddenly baffled, unrequite,
The planes wheel off in shaken flight—
The "all-clear" siren shrilling writes
An end to the hell of sound and light.

—Lt. John T. Weaver

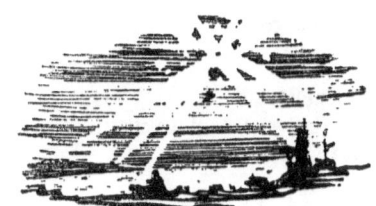

I HUNT TODAY

In bygone days, I used to hunt
The swiftly flying duck
And stalk through woods of birch and pine
To bag an eight-point buck.
I used to seek to flush the quail
That plump and wary fowl
And oft at night my roaring gun
Would end the coyote's howl.
I've faced the charged wounded moose,
I've felt the jaguar's claws,
I've faced the tiger's snarling growl,
The lion's hungry roars,
I've looked into the jaws of death,
And never had to pray,
But God, please give me courage,
I'm hunting "man" today.

—Sgt. A. Schneider

THE RANGERS *

Cool breath of evening
Softly gowned in velvet,
Diademed—
Hail Mary Full Of Grace;
Our Father Who Art In . . .
"Fall In!"
The jump-off:
"Ready. READY! here we go . . ."
Wonder if this time . . .

South of Rome, the beachhead:
Infiltrate, CISTERNA—cut the Appian way!
Tomorrow the day; tonight,
We march . . .
Veterans, battle-tried and steady
Rough hewn, weaponed, ready.
Rifles, bazookas, sticky grenades, bandoleers.
Rangers and Destiny nears—
Lead on soldiers here we go,
Through the ditches to Cisterna, traveling light,
March through the night,
Ghosts of Clark and Indian Rangers
Rogers and his rugged Rangers
Stalk the dark. They walk
Beside you, fellow Rangers—
Plod along easy . . . Quiet!

The silent night, cloud cloaked skies
Hide the danger that lies ahead.
The early dawn peers, stares
Where stalk the Rangers . . . Beware!
Here in strength the enemy lies
Poised for the kill.
But life as the rolling tide at will
Moves on. So the Rangers.

Near the edge of town
Flame stabbed, rock-walled, houses awake,
Mortars, artillery, tanks-blast and shake
To tear open the ranks of the Rangers.
Sunrise spells doom:
The dawn is now for the Rangers!
The Fight is on.

Men against tanks
Which line the road and banks;
Churn the fields; blast the woods
And the ditches! . . . Charge the tanks!
Rifles and blades, and sticky grenades.
Blast the treads: hurl yourself against tanks!
Ere your ranks are all gone
Barehanded men fight on.

Oh bloodied fields, ditches, woods,
Bloodied Rangers!
To the dangers of death you're not strangers.
Free men can die, must die
Till the danger that stalks
The Ranger is past.
Hark to the ghosts of Rogers and Clark:
Hark to the Rangers!
To the tomahawks that stalk
Until peace talks, and Freedom's light
Once more is bright
Over all the land.

They, too, marched through the dangers;
March on with THE RANGERS.

—F. Riley

*On January 30, 1944, two battalions of Rangers spearheaded an attack on Cisterna from the Anzio beachhead, then one week old. They were surrounded and cut off by the Germans. Only a handful escaped. The rest were killed or captured.

MONEY'S FUNNY

In Ireland I dealt pounds,
Bright silver florins smooth and round,
Sixpence, ha'crowns, battered shillings,
To know their value I was willing.
And so with zest I went to work
And learned them like a Dublin clerk.

In Africa I somehow shrank
From getting all the dope on francs,
For here the use of paper money
Reaches stages not so funny.
(The price of things, though fairly cheap)
Takes francs enough to fill a peep.)

But soon I bowed in concentration,
Learned centimes are for poor relations.
Now I know money like a banker
But still for U. S. dough I hanker.
(And yet when home, I'll bet I holler
"How many dimes are in a dollar?")

—Lt. E. G. Sayers

RAIN-SOAKED

Rain-soaked . . . my bed and my baggage,
It's happened before, or I'd cry:
But I think maybe it's worth it
For I feel so damn good when I dry.

—Lt. Rose C. Craig, ANC

BEN AHMED

Abou Ben Ahmed, may his tribe increase,
Make babies without surcease,
Send them out onto the rues
To shine American soldiers' shoes,
Rain or shine, they all must bum
Bon bons, choklot, and choon gum.

—T-3 Victor DaMaire

THE FRANC

If there's anything more exasperating to the average Yank
It's tryin' to understand the value of the shifty franc.
One day they push it up, the next they drop her
So that you never know if you're a millionaire or just a pauper.
Besides, all franc notes are either torn or pasted
Together in the middle and half your time is wasted
Matching pieces. Maybe it's because the French have awful temperaments
And like their money full of rips and tears and rents
Some guys will cram their franc notes in their wallet,
Which makes a nasty bulge upon their you-know-what-they-call-it.
But francs are most annoying in a poker game
Because the figures that you're using don't add up the same
And pretty soon you're broke. Or if you're winnin'
That stuff piles up so you've got no room to play in.
But what the hell, my francs are always spent—
So I'll still believe a franc is just one cent!

—T-3 John Willig

AH, SWEET MYSTERY

I wonder ef she's sittin' home a-waitin'
Or ef she's out a-gaddin' and a-datin'
My morale will go to ruin
Less'n I know what she's doin'
So I can stop this idle speculatin'.

I'd like to get me shut of all this doubtin'
And learn of our true love she's been a-floutin'.
Ef that wench o' mine back yonder
Is a-fixin' now to wander
I jist can't shut my mouth and set here poutin'.

My cotton pickin' haid I been a-wrackin'
Because this information I been lackin'
Ef I only knew it surely
That our love she's treating poorly
I wouldn't feel so guilty
'Bout my shackin'.

—T-3 Hal Brandels

CONVERSATION WITH A MULE

Now, Mule, you say you work too hard,
That you have a life of pain,
You never seem to get a rest
Through ice and sleet or rain.
You climb the highest mountains,
But remember I do, too.
You have four legs to take you home,
But me—I've only two.
And when our journey's over
And the time has come to eat,
A generous hand brings food to you
While you rest your weary feet.
I carry mine for miles and miles,
Have C rations every day,
Unless my luck's against me
And the cook throws me a "K."
And when it's time for us to sleep
There's one thing I can say,
I have to sleep on mountain tops
While you bed down on hay.
Now, Mule, would you take my place,
Even though you know you couldn't?
Would you be content with a life like mine?
You know darn well you wouldn't!

—Pvt. Richard Hiorns

THE MULE REPLIES

Dear Dick, you wrote and asked me,
If I'd trade my place with you
Because you think my life is free
And I've little work to do.
Well, brother, for your information
I work like hell to the very last,
And no matter what the situation
I still end up a sad, old ass.
Look at me in this same old hide,
Wouldst thou wear this ugly skin?
Would you daily drink from riversides
And forsake your whiskey and your gin?
And I can't get a small promotion
No matter if I work both hard and fast,
But you at the very slightest notion
Rise up to rank of private—yes—first class.
Now, Dick, after all I've told you,
If you still wanna be a mule,
Your request will not be considered,
For we won't accept so big a fool.

—Lt. Bernard Knighten

SITUATION NORMAL

I'm a six-foot-t'ree from Brooklyn,
A hunnert eighty when I'm bare.
Me hands is big as hammers
And me chest's a mat 'o hair.
I uster to be a boxer,
In de Dead End I wuz tops.
I wuz raised on lemon extract,
T'hell wid whiskey slops.
De Moider, Inc., boys wuz me pals,
I scare guys wid me puss.
To your sixty-four buck question,
I'm a typist, pal, t'ank youse.
—Sgt. Hank Chernick

SITUATION STILL NORMAL

Six years I pounded typist's keys
And copied shorthand notes with ease.
Before the Navy took me in—
A rag, a bone and dreadful thin.
No bulging muscles I display,
One hundred twenty pounds I weigh;
No beefy brawn on my physique—
I'm not a guy that makes gals weak.
My 'plaint runs quite the other way.
I slave with heavy tools all day.
Wracked with pain, my body bruised—
The Navy too, is all confused.
—RM 3c A. J. Betonti

THE PASSIONATE COMPANY CLERK TO HIS LOVE

(Apologies to Christopher Marlow)

Come live with me and be my love
And we will all pleasure prove
That make it grand to be with you
And TM twelve dash two-five-two.

We'll live by private special orders
Attached for rations, love and quarters
And ne'er surrounded by thy beauty
Shall I be present not for duty.

Of earthly bliss we shall have plenty
('Twill be writ on our Form 20)—
We'll need no CO's kind permission—
Our love will be "sans requisition."

We'll shop in no pool's bargain basements—
We'll fashion all our own replacements—
And as our company grows bigger,
We might surpass the TO figure.

'Twill be a blessing right from God
We'll go through life a well-trained squad
If these delights fulfill thy dream—
Then baby, thou art off thy beam.

—WO Henry J. Foner

TO HIDE A LOVE

Can I forget,
  You carved your name across my lonely heart?
  The vows and promises, that we would never part,
And—
  The days and hours we passed with idle talk;
  Your smile, your voice, and the swagger in your walk?

Can I forget,
  That once you were in my every reverie
  That now you never have a thought for me?
  Can I forget?
  It is what I ask.
  Perhaps I have,
  I'll wear this mask!

              —Lt. Sue Levins, ANC

ASSURANCE

I know now that maps can lie
For we are not so far apart.
Land and water may stand between
But they cannot barricade my heart.
I see you now as you were then—
Love, life and laughter in your face.
I hear your voice, I touch your hand,
I see your smile, I sense your grace,
Tonight, I watch beneath the stars
As my thoughts go o'er the sea,
How could I ever feel alone
When I know you wait for me.

            —Pfc. John Di Giorgio

EVEN THEN...

I love you on the battle edge
While life hurls forward as a means
To force the bristles of a wedge
Into the lives where Hatred leans
Upon the parapet with Death
Their cudgels ready and their whips
With hot and evil-jesting breath
And ice-inhaling sneering lips.
I love you when no thought keeps pace
With the assault of jarring steel.
When nerves snap with the bursting race
And bodies to its music reel.
There is no halting short to play,
No altar cloth for faith to touch.
Men rave through their atonement day
Rifles or sod is all they clutch.
But even then when madness beats
The burial drums from hole to hole;
When murder stamps its ripping cleats
In rhythm with each salvo's grave
Without the kindness of a tear
The softness of my love I save
And let it still the horror here.
—Pfc. Hans Juergensen-Steinhart

TASTE THE NIGHTBANE

In the tortured hours like these when all looms black,
(Unless it be the weird flame of our flak.)
I do not weave strange scenes I'll never live to see;
For Madame Fate with white cross spun my destiny.
I do not dream the poet's heartbreaking dream;
I have forgotten stardust and the sapphire gleam.
I have remembered but your wet-eyed face
When you did kiss me in our last embrace.
—Pvt. S. G. Sampas

SOLDIERS IN A CAFE

Some lean on tables in dark cafes,
Sip their wine, and through the clouds of smoke,
And milling flies, they gaze like stuffed men.

Some propped against the bar,
Talk in boastful tone of sordid nights in cheap hotels far
From the frightening noise, the pain and death,
The horror that stills your heart and takes your breath—
Some wonder why they're here, and some don't care;
Content with rank and rations, they plop their legs upon a chair,
Cock their caps and watch a Wac with vulgar stare—
Some with grand illusions look forward to the fight—
They're young, they flaunt their youth,
They've never seen a Gurka or a Goum,
Let them get drunk and swagger for soon
They'll have foreign earth for their tomb;
And some I've seen whose face you might assume,
Has lost its vigor, lost its bloom,
For they never again will be
The same in life as you and me.

Some lean on tables in dark cafes
Sip their wine, and through the clouds of smoke
And milling flies, they gaze
Like stuffed men and dream of home.

—Sgt. Hooker Goodwin

SCHOOLDAY SWEETHEART

She must have married someone rich and sports
Today undoubtedly a mink or seal.
To us who were her swains of lesser sorts
Who longed to hear her golden voice and feel
The velvet texture of her rosebud lips,
She was an ambulating, teasing dream.
When up the stairs her svelte form lightly trips
How raced the heart to see above the seam
Of her silk hose, the strip of bare that showed
Beneath her windblown flash of pleated skirt.
On her the gods all graces had bestowed
And at her side all other girls were dirt,
But on the matrix of my mind is sunk
Her image done in mink and seal and—*skunk*.

—Pvt. Samuel I. David

VON ARNIM'S LAST STAND *

Oh, Jurgen J. von Arnim wore an armor plated monocle,
But he couldn't see behind him—now, wasn't that ironocle?
He fought a rear guard action and he did it very bitterly,
With booby-traps and tellermines and gallant sons of Iterly.
"But tell us why?" the Eyeties cry,
"This fighting don't enrapture us.
"Advance! and show the fiendish foe
"We care not if they capture us!"
"They hit us with our Panzer down, but listen!" Jurgen pouted:
"If we go back I get the sack, so let us not be routed.
"We gotta face the ghoulish foe, no matter how they pommel,
"To cover the withdrawal of the dauntless Erwin Rommel."
"The Fox has run to cover, so just come along," said Ike,
"And we'll feed you compo rations—any letter that you like.
"And to soothe your wounded feelings, now that this here sea's our ocean,
"May I suggest the very best—a dash of Jurgen's lotion."

—T-5 Wallace Irwin Jr.

*Written and published the same day Von Arnim surrendered in Tunisia, ending organized Axis resistance in North Africa.

REMEMBER, DEAR

Oh, do not be a prude, dear
When I am far away,
Just have a lot of fun, dear,
Slip out each night to play.
The lads I left behind, dear
They, too, must have their fling,
Be sure to treat them kindly
And dance and laugh and sing.
The years are all too few, dear,
For reticence to wreck,
And should I find it true, dear,
I'll wring your pretty neck.
—Pfc. S. Kravchick

SUPPOSING

I surmise
That you'll surprise
My heart one day by saying:
"We are through . . .
I don't love you, Bill . . .
I was only playing."
I suppose
I'll take the dose
" 'Twas bitter," I will mutter;
But ere long
I'll get among
The girls and find another.
—Pfc. William L. Keyes

ALIBI

And if I kissed another, dear,
See not that I was kissing you?
Within my arms she disappeared
And to my true love I was true.

For love like rain falls every place—
It mattered not it wasn't you.
I kissed a girl, a pretty face,
Believe me, I was kissing you.
—1st Lt. Robert Modica

DOUBTFUL COMFORT TO A GI'S LOVE

Grieve not a bit if he plays awhile
With a foreign lass on some green isle;
In his secret soul she is just a whim
And you're the one who has all of him.
You have no cause, my dear, to be blue,
For in his heart he's not untrue;
For though faithless (to some) he may be,
He brought no heart when he crossed the sea.

—Cpl. Leroy C. Branch

KILLER'S VALENTINE

Is this the day of hearts
When love and lace hold sway?
The quarry this year is different
'Tis not for your heart I prey.

As Cupid shoots his arrows
To pierce your young, vain heart,
My glistening steel is sharpened
For missions after dark.

The excitement that I feel
As I go to seek the foe,
Is the self-same breathlessness
You gave me long ago.

—Cpl. Anthony Carlin

IN MEMORIAM

I can't recall your face or the color of your eyes,
Or sound of your voice when laughing 'neath the skies;
There would have been no ending,
If there hadn't been a start;
And yet you left a memory,
A faint murmur in my heart!

—Pfc. Samuel B. Shuman

COMPARISON

Reclining under an olive tree,
I recount your many charms,
And wonder what delights I see
In your lips, and legs and arms.

When artillery shells leave their certain scar
On earth's bright spring-time face,
My foxhole, I know, is cozier far
Than the warmth of your embrace.

I used to say there was a brilliance
In the sparkle of your eyes,
And I admired your body's resilience
When I caught you by surprise.

But aerial flares are brighter
Than the windows of your soul,
And there's more flex in the nerves of a fighter
As he creeps toward a Nazi knoll.

Your wit I considered sharp and nimble,
But I have been speedier still
When the hope of my heart could be held in a thimble
When hot lead plowed the hill.

But even though, on every score,
I doubt the worth of your charms,
I'd gladly change the brilliance of war
For your lips and legs and arms.

—T-5 R. W. Rubright

JAUNDICE IS JAUNTY

Classic color — saffron yellow
Sunday supper — lemon jello
Jonquils are yellow in the spring—
I'm just a yellow-tinted thing.
No pleasure this so please don't try it.
The doctor only mutters "Diet."
Dye it? My God, that's what they've gone and done!
Is it "Rit" or "Diamond"? Will it run?
I would rather have an appendectomy
Than this color which makes people object to me.
(I should say something at this point to please
The feelings of over-sensitive Chinese.)
I don't mind playing "The Yellow Peril"
But I hope no unwanted care'll
Creep up on me sight unseen,
For if I feel blue, it will show up "green."
And I picture with horror in my saffron head
What would follow "black and blue" and "seeing red."
So let all the world shun me; I know why—
I have my tongue in my cheek and a jaundiced eye!

—T-Sgt. Gene D. W. Edwards

WE WON'T FORGET

(Written under fire in a foxhole)

From olive groves near Venafro
Where ancient trees grow row on row
To surrounding mountains capped with snow—
How many died there?
We'll never know.

They traded the enemy shell for shell,
And took the place where comrades fell
Amidst the whistling, bursting hell—
How many died there?
We'll never know.

They are all brave both old and young
All are heroes, some unsung.
They gave their lives without regret—
These men, these men,
We'll ne'er forget.

—S-Sgt. Robert J. Dewey

OLIVE TREES KNOW AGONY

I heard the voice of the olive tree,
As we rested beneath its shade,
Whispering these words of hope to me
"Brave heart, be not afraid
"For we olive trees have memories
"Of former days of strife
"Good Jesus knelt beneath the shade
"Of our sister trees in Gethsemane.
"With sweat and blood a prayer he made
"For the fools you mortals be
"We olive trees have shared your pain
"Your griefs we do well know
"And when the peace returns again,
"We trees will live and grow."

—Maj. J. M. Colling

MINE LAYERS

"Ripeness Is All . . ."

Through nights of slanting rain
Marchers are planting pain;
Gardeners in boots
Plant tender seeds of mines
Where the dimmed flashlight shines,
Nursing the wire-vines,
Hiding the roots.
Boys in green raincoats scamper
Where grass will soon be damper
With sudden red.
Ripe, ripe the pain grows high
Sudden into the sky . . .
New-mown the new crops lie,
Earth's new-mown dead.

—Sgt. Peter Viereck

THE CO'S PRAYER

The moon is nearly down; the night is quiet,
Unbroken save by the soft trill of a bird
Soloist to the chorus of the marsh.

Around me in the woods the air is heavy
With breath of sleeping men—
Peaceful they lie
Dreaming not of the morrow and its dangers.

All day they growl and grumble, yet I know
Their childlike trust in me to lead them through
This grim trial of battle safely home—
A thousand hearts of loved ones far away
Depend on me, Lord, I am weak and human,
And cannot walk alone. Guide thou my way—
Steel thou my heart and let me keep the faith.

—Maj. E. H. Thompson

D-DAY INTROSPECTION

They call us brave,
But heroes draw from ruddier blood
And stalwarts feed on sturdier food,
And man's a slave,
A slave to ancient terrors uncontrolled
That damp our sometime courage with their cold
And ghostly fingers from the grave,
But now that we are snatched from peaceful life
And girt for strife
Bedecked in battle cloth and wearing heroes fame—
Why must we know this inward shame, this blame,
This fear of fear? Now let us save
Our birthright and our honour and our name—
Let us indeed be brave.

—Capt. Fulton T. Grant

BEACH PARTY

They are bathing in the strand,
And sprawling on the sand
At the fashionable sunlit Riviera,
But they float face down,
And the sands are painted brown
With the stains of these sun-bathers' lifeblood
For the dead now take their ease
By this loveliest of seas
Whose beauty and music are wasted.
They'll be buried, each by each,
And we'll tidy up the beach
For the benefit of those who will come here,
So the ladies may be gay and the men forget the day
When these waves were freighted with corpses—
But the dead will have their rest
For their slumber is blessed
And the burden of their battle is transferred.
—CWO Edwin J. Hoff

COTE D'OR

After the silent fears of our embattled century,
Another youth shall stroll this famed shore,
Another youth shall feel the wind's spill from the sea,
And stand enchanted by its soft onrushing roar.
But he shall be a freeman's son, intelligent and strong
Nurtured in faith, and worthy of heroic song.
—Pvt. S. G. Sampas

WOUNDED

. . . it feels so unreal falling here
without pain . . . without fear . . .
unable to move . . . alone on the ground . . .
furiously the battle rages overhead
weaving the sky with tracer thread!
—Capt. Milton E. Tausend

NON-COMBATANT

Today I walked a quiet little street,
An interrupted street. This rubble pile
The shards of home, plaster, stone and tile
Hiding the trinket, the hag with naked feet,
Seeks in the ruin to link the past with now.
Last night, I slept an interrupted sleep,
I woke from dreaming to the distant deep
Troubled roar of guns. From dreaming how
A bullet's interjection comes to you,
You champions of man! I know not why
I wear the uniform you glorify!
We give so little but our love we two . . .
Is parting for the time the only price
Asked us? Dear God, is this a sacrifice?

—Sgt. Ben Hobb

SKY PATHS

I wonder if my comrades
Now are walking through,
New sky-paths of laughter,
New sky-fields of blue.
If God reached down
And raised them high
(From crisply burning pyre)
Gave them brave new wings,
In freedom's breath to fly.
Or are their faces blackly twisted
(Numb with death's rough grasp)
Seeking still the swift release
From pain-racked, last, great gasp?

—Cpl. Charles E. Emley

SONGSTERS-SING!

Sing a song of El Guettar,
A song of Kasserine;
Sing a song of all that was,
Of all that might have been.
Sing a song of old Mateur
And sing a song of hate;
Sing a song, Salerno-born
And sing a song of fate.
And sing of old Cassino—
Of an Abbey on a hill—
And sing of old Nettuno
And a demon driving will.
Sing a song of all that was,
All that might have been,
But sing it strong in accents bold—
These things that have made us men!
—Lt. John V. Peterson

NIGHT RAID

The night sky flowers red
Above earth's tranquil bed
Where ack-ack tracer,
Like a red, garden racer
Steers the vaulting shell
Against the lies they tell.
In the feat of absolute
Destruction blooms the fruit
Of faith's resolve:
Men fight, they do not solve.
Men only stumble when they find
The answers of the mind—
But there is beauty, beauty here,
In silence, cold despair:
Night tiptoes high in outer space,
While fire assaults her candid face.
—Sgt. Roland De Munbrun

CORPORAL PETTIFER'S PEACE

Corporal Pettifer, crouched in a hole,
Wondered how war could be good for the soul;
Wondered if strife were a function of life,
Wondered and wished he were home with his wife.

Overhead bombs of the war-lords were screaming;
Nightmare ironical, lived without dreaming.
Deep in his crater, the mud to his middle
Pettifer wondered and pondered Life's riddle.

"What," he prospected, "will the cost of repair be
"To a great nation which, erstwhile so carefree,
"Now is left shattered, and battered and tattered,
"Struck by a man by whom nothing else mattered?
"Who will provide the lost babies with papas?
"Who now will cherish the statesmen sans toppers?
"Who will put food in the countless pinched bellies?
"What can be done for the husbandless Nellies?"

Thus mused the corporal. His spirit grew troubled
Thinking how often Man's efforts redoubled
Building our skyscrapers, railroads and bridges
Breeding fine babies or combatting midgets.

"How," wondered Pettifer, "can man create
"Proud habitations or buildings of state
"Only to labor still harder again
"Blasting them down until nothing remain?

"Scientists striving for bumper crops,
"Bootleggers trying to outwit the cops,
"Birth-control backers and CIO leaders,
"Brooklyn's famed Bums losing more double-headers.

"That happens to be our own pattern of life;
"What is the pattern of Global War's strife?
"Is it service, a means to an end?
"Blasting down homesteads we swore to defend."

Pettifer panted, his brain in a muddle,
Shivering bodily there in his puddle,
Groping for reason down there in the mud
Where some old Caesar had probably stood.
Sudden and loud like a cry in the night
Stark there came to him, an internal light . . .
Pettifer sensed he had answered the question:
War, is it useful or world indigestion?

"I'll write a book!" Thus the Corporal stated.
"I'll be a wonder!" he vociferated.
"I'll show 'em! I'll tell 'em. I'll make 'em all say:
"Elmer P. Pettifer, Corporal, 5A,
"World-loving genius, he knows how to fix it!
"The lock only yields when a smart fellow picks it.
"I'll be great! I'll be famous! Immortal or more!
"I'll be the first man to eliminate war!"

And out of his foxhole, determined to publish
The new rules of peace that he meant to publish,
He climbed. But sad as it be for our world,
The banner of Pettifer's Peace still lies unfurled.

And Mankind will never discover or know
Pettifer's plan to end Old World woe,
For just as, inspired, he leaped from his seat,
A sinister shadow, a mere hundred feet
From the place (and whom Pettifer didn't quite see) —
Tossed an iron-clad bottle of strong TNT.
The noise was immense. The bomb did its chore,
And Corporal P. would solve problems no more.
From his fate let us learn (and with what consternation)
That mending a world, the late Corporal's fixation,
Is a business too big for the mere human brain,
To wit: Our own forbears once tried it in vain.

Let us hope that the Corporal, though tender his years,
Has not vainly departed from this Vale of Tears,
Let us pray that our leaders, though human they be,
Will remember this tale and its sad guarantee
And remember its moral: one can't by just thinking
Make mankind stop fighting, nor drunkards stop drinking,
Nor can they by speeches, edict or decree
Do more for this world than did Corporal P.

—Capt. F. T. Grant

ARC DANCE

Wow, some crowd, ain't it?
Yeah, that band sure is smooth.
Say, that guy's right in the groove.
Look to your left a bit . . .
Yeh, I like to dance.
First one I have been to over here.
What, her? . . . not a chance
She moves like a truck-load of beer!
Wow . . . Pipe that gal, not bad, eh what;
Maybe she'll be a pal . . .
"May I have this fox-trot?
"What, you will? Say, that's swell!"
Humm, not a bad chassis for a French belle.
"Yeah, I've danced a bit, and
You're pretty good, too."
Oh, you'd rather go back and sit . . .
Well, thanks, I'll be seeing you . . .
"Hi, Joe, you doin' OK?"
. . . you guys got a truck goin' my way . . .
Yeah, swell dance, but I've gotta blow . . .
"Naw, Joe, not a chance, I really gotta go . . ."
Well, I'll be . . . raining: oh, well . . . what the hell . . .
. . . sure was nice in there for a spell . . .

—Cpl. Ben D. Rivlin

AMBITION

I've gone to six or seven schools
And learned an awful lot.
I'm an expert in almost everything,
I'm a Johnny-on-the-Spot.
But there's one thing I do not know,
It really bothers me:
What else is there for me to do
To make a P. F. C.?

—Pvt. Phil Krutchik

V-MAIL MABEL

Mabel McCarthy is going exotic,
Sending V-mail o'er the seven seas;
She's mighty passionate, highly erotic,
But her style remains strictly lend-lease.
She writes to a fellow in far-off Oahu,
Another one stationed on the Isle of Bahrein.
One is a GI with the ack-ack, Timbuctu,
And one an MP on the shores of the Thyne.
She vows her love in sizzling expressions,
The V-mail machines fairly hum,
The celluloid crackles like heated C-rations,
These fables by Mabel leave 'em dumb.
Just in case these fellows in unpronounceable places,
Fail to come home or write her each day,
She keeps in the hole a couple of aces,
Four-effers, you know, from Pottstown, Pa.

—Pvt. Walter Coatell

TO A CIVILIAN INSECT

I wrote . . . "My Darling," and I paused
And cursed beneath my breath,
And swung a potent left hand
That dealt a crushing death.
"Good evening, dear," I wrote and then
I paused and swung again . . .
Missed and cursed at Africa
Whose insects bother men.
I watched that fly soaring away,
Gleefully saw him light
On polished, pate of colonel
And that made things all right.
Flies—you may plague me as you will
And though I will never thank
You for your bothering ways
You're cleverly free from rank.

—Lt. John V. Peterson

NOT IF . . . BUT WHEN

Not if . . . but when
We meet again
And the hearts of men are free
Once more:
Not if . . . but when
In your eyes again
I see what I was fighting for:
Not if . . . but when
In my arms again
You whisper the words I adore
Then my dreams of the long battle nights
Will come true in the reality of you:
Our love will be again
Not if . . . but when.

—Pvt. F. J. Stebbing

ONE TALENT

Life is not the glory it once was
When I had both your love and you.
Now I must live with just your love
But that was more wealth than once I knew.

I know I fail you if I rise at dawning
And turn from sunrise in the sky,
I know the fine contempt you taught me
For those too small to live . . . or die.

The day that ends and finds no added treasure,
A job well done, a new friend made, a poem;
Some bit of beauty, wisdom, truth to carry home
Lessens my stature, shrinks my total measure
Turns our love's promise into a lie.

Dearest, I don't deserve the love you're giving
If war should dull the edge that love gives living.

—Sgt. Ben Hobb

UNENDING TIME

What should I do but love you? You who fill
My waking thought, my days, the last sweet hour
Before slow sleep soft as a summer shower
Comes on me and my turbulent thoughts are still.
What should I do but love you? You the ill
Unending time have ended, when a dour
Dull rout of nights on empty nights did cower
And empty days worked out their aimless will.
Yet still my heart is weary. It has seen
The bitter wreck of love unwarranted
Time's waste, despair, the leisured death of life
And all its beauty crumbling in the strife
Of inner conflict. Can the tree once dead
Put on again its fresh and April green?

—Sgt. Tom Evel

TRILOGY

J'attendrai

These be
Three sweet eternities:
Your low voice,
Your adoring eyes,
The touch of your lips . . .

Rubato

How sweet
Are remembered kisses
And fickle love
Postering
Like a slave . . .

Coquette

I have mended
My heart
Into a crazy quilt
Because of you and you
And you . . .

—Lt. S. Vezmar

RESPITE

Today's the day! Occasion great!
To spring from bed I cannot
  wait.
I'm up at dawn, so's not to miss
One single molecule of this—
MY DAY OFF.
   —Pvt. Dorothy E. Dower

I WONDER

If you composed the equal of
The letters that you claim
And sent them overseas to me
And I received the same,
I'd have enough to cover up
The plaza in Oran
And still be able, I am sure,
To fill a GI can.
But very much to my regret
They never come to me,
And as you told me once before
They may get lost at sea.
The only thing that I can say
If this is truly such,
Ol' Davy Jones must find it nice
To hear from you so much.
   —Cpl. Paul R. Campbell

OBSERVATION

The things in life we deem most delectable
Are all too often "unrespectable."
   —S-Sgt. Gray Wilcox

DIARY OF A NURSE

I dreamed I'd see this country,
If I ever had the luck;
But in my wildest fancies,
It was never made by truck.

Nurse Nightingale before us
Carried candles through the mist;
The modern maid of Mercy
Totes a helmet in her fist.

Nostalgic waves encompass me
Though I'm still patriotic;
Tonight, my dear, I long to see
A land that ain't exotic . . .
                —Lt. Rose C. Craig, ANC

RESPECTFULLY SUGGESTED

A happier way, it's one of my tenets,
Of answering all of our gripes,
Is to cut apart some second lieutenants.
And pass them around—as stripes.
              —T-5 John Radosta

WAR SUMMARY

Hostilities
Aren't subtleties.

That's all chum,
That's the po-um.
        —Lt. David E. Diener

THE WAR MAKES MEN, AND OTHER ASSORTED PRODUCTS

When war is through, they notify us,
The Army means to un-GI us,
For, after all this rough campaigning,
We'll need civilian basic training.

I never thought they'd undermined me
So bad that now they have to find me!
I have to be repatriated
Before I'm re-United Stated!
—Pfc. Henry B. Mackey

SUPPLY

I drew a jacket yesterday
And still am throwing tags away;
When I am sure de-tagging's done,
I'm bound to find another one.
I worked last night 'til very late.
Detected, pried off twenty-eight.
There's something tickling at my spine:
B'gad, I'll bet it's twenty-nine.
—Ens. Bob Haakenson

NOT IN BROOKLYN

I'm glad that I'm American,
I'm glad that I am free
I wish I were a little pup
And Hitler were a tree!
—T-5 E. W. Botten

LETTER TO AMERICA

We are waiting the long days to D-day, the last hours to H-hour, the minutes before zero, counting the time,
We are waiting in canvas tents above the beaches,
The beaches we took in November as a beginning to these days,
The beaches we took in the march to the east,
The beaches we took in the last weeks at Cape Bon.
And now we are waiting and looking across the sea and running the ramrod through our M-1s and counting our rifle clips and watching the flick of sun on our bayonets.
We are well, America, and we are ready. We are waiting for the signal.
In November we came to a continent with a Blue Book
Telling us what to do, what to say, how to say it,
But when we hit the beaches we forgot the Blue Book and we did it our own way, said it our own way and in our own voice.
And the people were glad to see us and we made ourselves at home.
We came here with weapons that did not weigh us down but made us stronger:
With the howitzer of the Maine farm on our backs, the good soil, and the corn stalks and the cool rains,
With the mortar of the Shenandoah Valley, and HE shells of red oak, white pine, and blue rivers,
We carried hand grenades of Scranton coal and Alabama cotton bolls
And battering rams of Oregon sequoia.
Thinking of home while we fought in the wadis and djebels of Tunisia, new thoughts came to us and we remember them:
The world must build a new house, America, a house big enough for all the peoples to live in
(For we on the beaches of Africa are waiting now to splinter the old house, crash in its weak rafters, rip up its rotten floorboards, open it up to the sky.)
There will be many residents in the new house, America: the British who fight with endless determination; the Chinese who fight with the strength of generations: the Russians who fight with iron faith in their vast land; the French who fight to bring their land to life; the conquered peoples of the slave states, saddled with quislings, betrayers, spies, waiting now to get the fighting chance; and the people of the Axis, who must be brought once more into the house.
A house so great will need firm foundations, America, and the foundations we remember in your hills and valleys: the concrete of the structure needs firm lumber from your tall, benevolent trees to make the form; water from cool and tolerant streams to make the mix; granite from your deepest quarries for toughness and strength; and hardening by your warm and overseeing sun.
It is time to begin these foundations now, time to draw up the blue print.
The blueprint, America, must be drawn to the right proportions this time.

—T-Sgt. Milton Lehman

GI PROFILES

The GI

The GI is a wordy bird,
 His letters really should be heard:
By day and night, he'll always write
The world's all wrong, but he's all right.
"These guys with brass don't know the score,
Why don't they let me plan the war!"

The Moocher

The moocher has a greedy paw,
The longest reach you ever saw,
And when he gets a box, he'll hide
Until he's stuffed it all inside.
But when others get the same
He considers them "fair game."

The Goldbrick

The Goldbrick really hates to work
And every detail tries to shirk
But here's the joke, and listen well,
In ducking jobs, he works like hell!

Sad Sack

"Sad Sack" is an Army term,
Signifying you're a germ.
Though "jerk" conveys a mental lack
There's nothing sadder than a "Sack."

—Pvt. Frank Robichaud

GREENHORNS

You still Lux-ing undies, honey?
You've been doing that all day.
That's not tattle-tale, dumb bunny
That's just honest GI gray.

—Lt. Rose Craig, ANC

LET ME

Let me dream tonight
I'm tired, let me rest;
Give me fingertips across my brow,
My head against your breast.
I want the sedative of voices,
Soft . . . the peace of years gone by;
The happy smile of lovers
With faces to the sky.
I want to take hold of a memory,
The forgotten flutter of a fife:
Breathe into our yesterdays
The breath of love and life.

—Cpl. Harry Olive

SOLITAIRE

Solitaire!
All I do is play solitaire.
I don't even comb my hair
Since you said you didn't care:
Red card . . . black card . . .
King, Queen . . . Ace!
They all look like your sweet face . . .
Red card . . . black card . . .
Nine . . . Ten . . . Jack!
Honey, won't you please came back?
Don't you care?
What's happening over there?

—Pvt. John Di Giorgio

FIRST LOVE

What am I lonesome for?
America! Her soil and soul,
In peace and love. Make sure her lawns
Are tended well. I'd love to see
Her face so fair that nothing else
Could be behind but purity.

—Pfc. Harold S. Peterson

MISSING IN ACTION

"To Young Hutch, USA RAF"

No longer will you penetrate
The heavens in your chase
For human game, lay prostrate
His crawling legions and waste
All gain in his fight: somewhere,
As a wounded bird, you lie
Helpless upon earth in despair.
Oh child of youth! We cry
At our loss; we curse the sky,
For having taken you away—
The craft you used to fly—
War and Death a game to play . . .
How quiet this hour, the skies are bare
Though I hear you laughing everywhere.

—F-O Doug Wallace

LAW IN MY HANDS

These two poor futile hands of mine aren't strong,
For they are thin, reflective, pale and long;
Ten fingers made to hold a dreamer's pen,
Ten servants made to grace a poet's den.
At first these hands of mine could find no sense
In acts of dirt, and hate and violence.
Full facile in the art of word's allure,
The battle's duty found them slow, unsure,
And though I'm sure they'll never have the skill
In handling things designed to maim or kill,
These two weak tools are pledged a job to do
They are pledged to champion the good and true.
These hands are dedicated to the cause
Of punishment for breakers of the laws,
Of freedom and equality of lands
And for this, the law was placed into my hands.

—Pvt. Marvin Shaw

TRIBUTE

Far out in the Mediterranean
Many miles from either shore,
There's a bomber crew that's sleeping
'Neath the mighty water's roar;
No mounds of clay are heaped up o'er them,
No poppies grow 'round their graves
But there's a mound for every soldier,
In the vastness of the waves.

—S-Sgt. Jimmie Church

GOUM

Where oleanders bloom
The fierce warrior Goum
Laid down his precious life:
... he cut off the head
Of the enemy dead
With his curved Konmia knife.
Where the rains weep
And the winds sweep
The red dust over all:
The blood red rose
Sheds peace on those
Who answered the battle call.

—Lt. Liberty Campbell

WINGLESS VICTORY

I dreamed I died last night,
The earth was cold and opened wide
To intercept my heart's last flight
As it raced on the bloody tide
Of life's last sullen act. I died!
No plummeting to earth in flame,
No crimson meteor spelled my name;
Unchartered skypaths then I tried;
But ... cruel the Gods an airman bound
And made him die upon the ground!

—F-O Doug Wallace

GRIPE POEM

Hey, move over
Give me a little room
To a guy who doesn't
Give a rhyme;
Who can't scan;
Who doesn't know feet
From elbow high.
So I can't be poetic
About things energetic
When I got gripes
Enough for ten poems.

—Cpl. Max Greenberg

ENIGMA

Which came first, the egg or the hen?
Puzzled a lot of prewar men;
But will someone ever live to tell
Which came first, the whine or the shell?

—Pvt. John P. Nantell

TIMID WOLF

My howl is but a dismal screech,
My leer is a sickly grin;
Can it be I've mouse blood,
Or lack of vitamins?
How gay 'twould be to join the pack,
And hunt the quarry sleek,
But alas! Alack! when at the kill,
My growls would be but squeaks.
Yes, gay would be the merry chase
With guile a growing lore.
But I shall *dream* my conquests
Then I'm sure of perfect scores.

—Lt. John A. Weaver

WRITTEN AT THE GRAVES OF KEATS AND SHELLEY

The surging crowds have swelled the roads of Rome,
And seeking inspiration blindly sweep
Through Colosseum, Forum, and the deep
And musty Catacombs, and awesome dome
Of Peter's Church, and slowly lumber home—
Well drugged with old illusions worn and cheap
Like glutted beasts who seek their midday sleep.
Go Pilgrim, rather where the cypress moan
Is borne by mourning winds that softly wail
The dirge of Nature for the sons below:
Cut off too soon upon their silvered trail
So strewn with gems, that we can only know—
Immortal hands have furled great Shelley's soul
And garlanded our Keats his god-like brow!

—Lt. Irving E. Rantanen

TO DANTE AND BEATRICE

This is the bridge. Dante stood in this place
And caught a fire that flamed Firenze town
Forever, more consuming than her face
That dimmed the burning crimson of her gown.
Here Beatrice half-looked and but half-meant
That first timid covert glance of love
That made of Dante furnace of torment
All lovers since have wept in pity of.
Now here stand I and watch the crowd,
Scourged by the cruel shepherding of war,
The famine-eaten faces, the eyes loud
With hatred never known by man before—
O Dante, touch to them the flaming sign,
O Beatrice, they need of love divine.

—Pvt. Donald J. Titus

KEEPSAKE

I carry a well worn photograph
Next to my heart. Its case is torn
And dirty, yet your smile, your laugh
Is there just the same, unworn
By cares and time. Only your clothes
Are dated . . . the fancy painted scene
Was not real . . . youth still flows
Through the cheeks with sheen
Of health, luxuriant summer peace
In the days when the world was sane.
I can't recall—was it Cannes or Nice?
Will such carefree days return again?
I'll put away the photo-old, torn and bent
Along with the telegram the War Department sent.

—F. O. Doug Wallace

ATLANTIC CHARTER

You bear the lamp of freedom as a God,
Inviting reason to accept its rays
And disregard for good war's iron rod,
The use of which betokens evil days.
You offer peace upon a pedestal
And prize it as a jewel without price,
Encouraging in turn the tyrants' fall
Who, grouped together, caused this sacrifice
Of human lives whose suns had yet to set
'Ere death could claim their fate—alloted years—
A task forever thriving on regret
For something past when only nothing nears,
Unlike the hope you spring before our eyes
Which dazzles us with Truth and not with lies!
—Pvt. Francesco Bivona

AND NOW--OCTOBER

(Winning poem of ARC Poetry contest)

October now—and soon
You will mulch the flower bed,
Tie back the rambling rose bush
And watch for the maple's red.
The house will have its changes;
Chairs emerge from summer white—
And logs will wait by the fireplace
For some frosty starlit night.
October now—tonight perhaps
You will sew upon that heavier dress—
The while your mind on jelly stores—
Or hazarding some domestic guess.
The clock will tick within the room
And October roll its way—
But the world of two is waiting
For my homecoming day.
—Sgt. Virgil Scott

TANK MEN

Out of their tombs they crawl
Weird, misshapened men.
Faces tattooed with cordite,
Eyes sullen and red.
Nine hours in the tanks
Have made them kin to the dead.
—Capt. Milton E. Tausend

THE NEWS

I am tired of listening to the news—
A voice from nowhere tells me nothing.
By mathematical logic it has deduced
If we are increased as the enemy's reduced
That we will win the war. Hence I choose
Not to listen to the "News."
I'd rather be a pagan suckled in a creed outworn
Than be baptized by BBC from dusk to dawn.
      —Lt. "Chick" Rainear

VERONA

Dante found peace in Verona,
When Florence sent him away;
But Verona's no longer a refuge,
Bombs fell upon it today.
San Micheli's noble city,
An architectural boast,
Was a military target,
Prey to a Fortress host.
Verona's lofty cypresses,
Among the country's finest trees,
Never before knew iron hail,
In all their centuries.
War's no time for gallantry,
Yet deeply we regret,
That we must assault
The city of Juliet.
Sleep, tragic Giulietta,
Dream as best you may,
We disturb no nightly tryst,
Because we come by day.
    —Pvt. Edwin J. Barrett

SEASON'S GREETINGS

"Opus To My Draft Board—!"

Know all men by these presents
That a jury of your peers
Awards you greetings pleasant
As the Christmas season nears.
You put us where we are today,
We tender you our thanks.
A million games we've learned to play—
Like hide-and-seek with tanks,
And blind-man's bluff with hand grenades,
And hop-scotch with a mine,
Plus many dandy dress parades
We've had behind the line.
So greetings, Draft Board buddies who
Have filled our lives with cheer.
This festive verse we share with you—
But wish, of course—that you were here!

—Cpl. W. S. Westcott

CHRISTMAS EVERY DAY

Your packages, so gaily wrapped recall
A thousand scenes from former Christmas seasons;
The well-stocked stores, the throngs of shoppers, all
In festive mood, quite unconcerned with reasons;
The Christmas trees, their colored lights aglow;
The tinsel, baubles, candles, ribbons, wreaths;
And further back, the child-like urge to know
The contents of the odd-shaped gifts beneath.
It seems a shame to open them so soon,
With scenes so far removed from all this past.
I'd like to save them, but there is not room;
And, spread apart, they will much longer last.
Besides, I mean the wrappings to make gay
The washerwoman's child, come Christmas Day.

—Cpl. R. W. Lovett

IN CAROLINE

When it's November time in Caroline
And the sky is smoky blue,
And the woods are trailing crimson
And they're calling me and you.
And the paw-paw's getting mellow
And the nuts fall pit-a-pat,
And the squirrels are getting sassy
And the possum's getting fat.

When it's November time in Caroline
And the fields are rusty brown.
With their river marge of yellow
And their coverlet of down,
And the quails are plump and tempting
And the pheasant's getting fat.
And they're waiting there a' scratching
And a-wondering where I'm at.

When it's November time in Caroline
And the moon is melon red.
And the hounds are making music
And the possum's playing dead.
And the rabbits and the groundhogs
And the coons are getting fat,
While I'm over here in Italy
And they wond'ring where I'm at.

When it's November time in Caroline
And the air is so alive
And it gives a chap a feeling
That he ought to up and jive.
Oh, I wish I had my shot gun
And my bacon and my pan—
I'd just up and leave this country
For a while and be a man!

—Pfc. James D. Ammons

FORBIDDEN DRINK

"No-one will milk a cow within
The area," so reads the sign;
Since drinking milk is such a sin,
Cheer up, we'll get along on wine.

—Cpl. R. W. Lovett

LOGIC

A T-4 proudly wears three stripes
T-5s wear two, the hicks,
So logically the guy who wears
One stripe is a T-6;
A barren stripeless khaki arm
Perforce would be T-7
Which in perverted minds is held
To be the GI heaven.
The rank that I am bucking for
(Oh, Lord! please get this straight)
Is stripeless, un-GI, carefree,
Civilianized, T-8.

—Capt. Ed Rust

BUMPS

A sweater lass I chanced to pass,
Smiled sweet, I stopped to question
A name abreast one side her chest
Was writ with good intention.
In letters fair, embroidered there,
She parried, "by her mother"—
"If one, my pet, is Harriet—
What do you call the other?"

—T-4 Bill Weil

TWINKLE, TWINKLE

Twinkle, twinkle, little flare
I see you hanging in the air
And wish to hell you'd go away
Before the bombs begin to play.
—T-Sgt. Bob Wronker

LITTLE BANKROLL

Little bankroll, ere we part
Let me press you to my heart.

All the month I worked for you,
Slaved and toiled and sweated, too.

Little bankroll, in a day
You and I will go away

To some gay and festive spot.
I'll return . . . but you will not.
—Pvt. G. G. Sybert

TRUCK DRIVERS

A female hitchhiker from Bari
Had legs that made truck drivers tari
It wasn't the beauty
That kept them from deauty
They just were exceedingly hari.
—Lt. Owen Cooper

OBLIVION

What is this word 'death,' that falls
On the thought of life like the toll
Of oblivion, which one day calls
In the darkness and beckons the soul
To come and forget, and what does it mean
To join hands with the spirit, dumb, unseen?

For these, they say, are the garland joys
Of dying, to be wreathed in the smoke
Of funeral embers, beyond the noise
Of a world in flames, to soak
In the blood of a hero's battle fire;
But not for me the laurels, nor the pyre.

I know only what to feel,
To sense what is close, in the nearness
Of a loved one's flesh to seal
The breath of this life with the dearness
Of her kisses on my lips, here
In our laughter, though in pain and fear:
For our hearts care not for death, nor crave
The forgetfulness of going out to our grave.
—T-4 Lawrence W. Shenfield

THOUGHT

Like dark wings darting seaward
Are thoughts that flit the mind,
And shadows of brain afterward,
Their reasons we try to find.

Why do they come to man
From the secret beds of time,
Since God bespoke and life began,
Your thoughts and mine?
—Sgt. Lewis P. De Reimer

REQUEST

Reach for the moon, my son,
Which I have placed within the sky,
And when you have it in your hand
Affix the ray within your eye
For all to see.
Reach for the star, my son,
Which I have hung with utmost care,
And when you have it in your grasp
Sprinkle its dust upon your hair
For all to see.
Reach for the dream, my son,
That I have dreamed these many years,
And keep its music in your heart,
Its laughter in your tears.
Do this for me.
—S-Sgt. William Callahan

GI LOVE LETTER

My Dear:
 Long have I sought
 For words that will declare
 My love for you.

And often,
 Have I thought
 For lines by which to swear
 My love for you.

In song
 Have I brought
 This unenvied voice to bare
 My love for you.

With deeds
 Have I fought
 To express this cherished dare:
 My love for you.
—Sgt. C. W. Carroll Jr.

TO GENERAL McNAIR AND SON
(Por Patria Mori)

Not long ago, sir, you had made a speech
A salute to the mothers of the men
Who serve the "queen of battles."
It struck us as it came o'er the loudspeaker's strident tones
Akin a declamation on the field of battle
Hon'ring the mother of the men
Who fight as men up to the struggle's end.
Now you lie dead on Britt'ny's rocky shore—
Your son lies dead on Guam's coral strand!
Now whom did you salute? Your mother—
Or all mothers of the land?
The mothers of the Infantry, en masse,
Whom you had honored as was their just due
Return now that salute—
And smartly, too.

—T-5 Max J. Ritter

CHANGE

Where once we clambered, we twain,
Some wild flower will bloom;
And in the fox-hole where we have lain
The thrush will make its room.
The horizon against which we bled,
Will silently glow some day;
I shall not fear to raise my head
And stand upright and pray.

—Maj. Leon W. Goldberg

TO THE MASTER RACE

(A tribute to the hospital ship, St. David, sunk off Anzio by Germany's GLORIOUS Luftwaffe)

Project not your might against defenders
Of a fortress, armed to kill, to render
Your legions useless as a bobbing cork
Swimming in your own blood running dark
In rivers from the fight. Steel not
Tanks and guns, against men and arms, but blot
From the sea mercy ships: breeders of sanity
In a world devoid of love—man's inhumanity
To man such ships destroy! Go now, bomb, fire:
The holocaust foreshadows your own funeral pyre!

—F. O. Doug Wallace

YOU ARE MORALE

All happenings of earth
Would be subject for mirth,
You can bet.
Pain, famine and fire,
Or the consequences dire
Hold no threat,
And my courage would stay,
In fact, day by day,
I'd grow bolder,
If each night in my bed
I'd find your pretty head
On my shoulder.

—Capt. Louis Reese Jr.

TELL ME, POP

"Tell me, papa, how was life
"When you were young and had no wife?"
"Listen son, it was rife—
" 'Twas rife, 'twas rife.

Rife with horses, bookies, phones,
Red dog, poker, blackjack, bones;
Whiskey, cognac, vino, hops,
Taverns, poolrooms, three-ball shops.

Listen, sonny, I had fun
Until I turned twenty-one.
Then a maid with dimpled knees,
With kisses like an April breeze,
With ankles formed to smite the eyes,
With hair aflame like sunset skies,
Slyly stole away my life,
Made me take her for my wife,
My wife, my wife—!

—Lt. S. Weinstein

UNPRINTABLE THOUGHT

("The type of woman who approaches you on the street in Italy and says: 'Please give me a cigarette' isn't looking for a smoke."— Soldier's Guide to Italy.)

I frankly haven't seen as yet
A babe who mooched a cigarette
While one who would, and English speak,
Is surely something quite unique.

If a smoke ain't what she's a-lookin' for
It must be gum; she wants a chaw.
Hey there, Bud, just cut that winkin'
It can't be printed what yer thinkin'!

—T-Sgt. Bob Wronker

THE WEAKER SEX

There's a practical problem on my mind
Which makes me ponder and vex,
I have been trying so hard to find
How weak is the weaker sex.

If by the weaker sex we mean the "she's"
And most men claim it's true,
Then the stronger sex must be the "he's,"
But there's my Waterloo.

Now, enlighten me, Oh, man, so wise
If you be as strong as they say
Why, then, when heated disputes arise
It's she, not you, who gets her way?

On woman's power I loath to linger
Or to speak of the souls she threw aside;
Why she has twisted giants around her finger
And forced stronger men to suicide.

I urge you men to reassert your power
As you did in days gone by,
For your authority wanes by the hour
And your cup is running dry.

—Pfc. Larry Cohen

THREE CHEERS FOR THE APO

Why is it that the mail I write
Gets home okay, without a blight?
But all the mail that's sent to me
Takes ten damn months to cross the sea?

—S-Sgt. Gray Wilcox Jr.

THE PEOPLE SPEAK

To Fish and Nye
We say good-bye,
Isolationists
Become vacationists.

—Pvt. Edward Galowitz

HOME TO A HOSS

Dere's a hoss o' mine down on a Texas range
Roamin' 'round the countryside.
He ain't much of an animal
'Cause he's thin, rheumy, saggyspined and kinda pretty old.
But he's my hoss, every twisted bone o' him.
Now, some soldiers are goin' home to wives,
Some are goin' home to sweethearts and mothers,
But me—I'm goin' home to my li'l Texas range
And I'm gonna sell this bony hoss o' mine:
I'm gonna get rid o' him.

—Sgt. Harry Shershow

HAPPY BIRTHDAY, BUD

I storm my friends with festive lyrics
I never miss a birthday home,
I hack away at panegyrics
For each occasional—lo! a poem.
Must my ego be suppressed?
It becomes me not, such modesty.
This difference must be redressed.
Today's my birthday: here's to me.

—Bud Arnold, Y 2c

WAR WIDOW

So what . . . if I vowed to him—
My life is not to please his whim.
I loved him, yes . . . but he's away.
Does that mean I shan't sing today?
Oh, life is short, let's make it sweet.

Come, darling, I have dancing feet.
I promised him that I'd be true,
But waiting is so hard to do.
You know . . . it's really tough on me,
He's far away in Italy.

That's okay, Babe . . .
Enjoy your merriment
When I return . . .
Who's going to pay the rent?
—Pvt. Chad Cobb

NIGHT CAPPED

A GI who camped near Bologna
Sent home to his wife a kimogna
She wrote him next week
And called him a sneak—
For it reeked with Eau de Cologna.
—S-Sgt. James I. Goodrich

HAPPY SOLDIERS

It's easy to pick California soldiers,
They are not in the least downhearted;
They're smiling because they're right at home,
Now that the autumn rains have started.
—Cpl. Harry P. Volk

ARE YOU NERVOUS IN THE SERVICE?

Are you nervous in the service, Mr. Jervis?
Do you wish that you were anywhere but here?
As the shells begin a-squealing
Do you get that empty feeling
That your life has been shortened by a year?
There are times at night when "butterflies" are fallin'
That you really wonder what it's all about.
Then a shell comes helter-skelter
And you dive for nearest shelter,
And once more you curse the dirty, lousy Kraut.
Are you nervous in the service, Mr. Jervis?
Are you frantic—don't know quite just what to do?
Well, please don't let it getcha,
For you'll find, if time will letcha,
That, though you're nervous, I am nervous, too!

—Pvt. Eddie Bendityky

COMING CLEAN

The Army will not make you rich—
So runs the song with bugle.
Yet in Algiers I saved my pay
By being very frugal.
"Why didst not bring that dough to me?"
My wife will ask suspiciously,
With raised eyebrow and lurking thought
I spent my money viciously.
"I was not gay," I'll say, "nor could
I buy you gems and scarabs.
My money went for laundry bills,
Charged me by many Arabs."

—Maj. Fairfax Downey

THE CORONA CAMPAIGN

Our Irish was up when our wave hit the beach.
We flipped back the bolt and threw one in the breech,
Expecting a welcome of hot, screaming lead,
But "Report of Change due, please," met us instead.
We struggled with ammo and gas by the ton,
And dug enough foxholes for every last one,
Expecting a Heinkel or two up our way,
But no—"Your Status Report's due today."
At last a barrage!—of publications.
Reports, requisitions and recommendations,
Copies quintuplicate volley and thunder,
Letters and circulars bury us under.
So when we return from this war (soon, Lord, please!)
And our inquiring offspring climb up on our knees
With embarrassing questions like, "Papa, old chap,
Just how did you conquer the German and Jap?"
We'll spout, with chest out, and heroic leer on,
"My child, I replied by indorsement hereon!"

—Capt. J. H. Critton

*WHEN DUTY CALLED**

We've laid aside our peaceful tasks,
We've packed our kits and gone to war.
We loved those things we left behind,
But loved our country even more.

And though we lie in some strange land,
Forgotten perhaps, by all but God,
We rest in peace because we know
Transgressors' heels shall never grind
Our country's flag into the dust.

We know, because we made it so,
The lad whose hands have milked the cow,
Whose hands have guided straight the plow;
He did not shirk his country's call,
But gladly gave his life, his all.

We loved the murmur of the brook
That flows between the mountain slopes;
The golden moon that softly smiled
As if he shared our secret hopes.

We loved the whisper of the rain
Upon the roof tops overhead;
The gleam of sun upon the snow.

We sacrificed these things we loved
To keep our flag forever free.
We know, because we made it so.

The lad whose hands made tools of steel,
Whose hands have held the big truck's wheel;
He did not shirk his country's call,
But gladly gave his life, his all.

—An American Sergeant

---

*The above poem by an American sergeant was found among his personal effects and forwarded to The Stars and Stripes by his commanding officer. A waist gunner with a Flying Fortress crew, the sergeant was killed April 17, 1944, while participating in a bombing raid of the NAAF.

REVERIE

I shall be coming back to you
When winter turns to spring;
When sunshine warms the heart again
And stirs each living thing.

I shall be knocking at your door,
I'll look into your eyes;
And life again will seem to us
A beautiful surprise.

The garden swing will beckon us,
The woods and lakes will call;
And when the sun goes down, the night
Will loan her starry shawl.

Our hands will touch and we shall walk
Familiar paths once more.
For us the world again will be
The way it was before.

The moon will rise above the clouds
To smile his welcome then;
And I shall take you in my arms,
And kiss your lips again.

—Pvt. Russell Brown

AND THEN ...

I shall forget?
Perhaps ... if you can tell me when
I shall forget!
Or, if you have the answer, let
Me know how memories once aroused are stilled.
Grant me this ... then,
I shall forget.

—Sgt. O. D. West

BEYOND ALL POWER

Delicately thought up prose ...
The best book written and who knows
In all the rest to come,
Nothing could ever be penned
About this love which knows no end.
And he who thinks that words can say
That which makes me care this way
Would really be ...
Just as sane as those who know
What makes the little posies grow!

—Pfc. D. James Sawyer

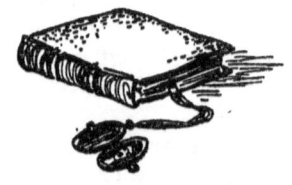

LITTLE THINGS

Of little things the past is made—
A spot beneath an elm tree's shade;
A shabby house, a drowsy street,
The drug store where the gang would meet.

The little church on Spruce and Main,
The fragrance of a summer rain;
The courthouse park, where cannon's roar
Still echoes from another war.

A father's voice, a mother's face,
A sweetheart's smile and gentle grace.
How precious in their common way
Are small events of every day.
My heart forgets the span of sea
When little things come back to me.
—S-Sgt. Virgil Scott

DESIRE

Of all the gifts
God has to give
I only ask
But one—to live.

To live it—
An abundant life
And by my side,
My lovely wife.
—Capt. William A. Anderson

FOURS IN OLIVE DRAB *

Asleep In Africa

Gnarled wires hung in cross-wise spread
Crude boards for posts and frame, all bare
Such trash my love and once a bed.
I know because I missed you there.

War Cry

Of all the things I yet miss
Most keen your lovely evening kiss;
And all the war that I yet face
Weighs less than loss of your embrace.

Breakers At Anzio

Breakers on Anzio beach come home,
Languishing, hungering, ever and more
Towards the cool sands they will bathe in foam
Amorous, even like me for my shore.

Infantry

There seldom are the glory and the fame
Or marches, clamor, bugles, drums and flags;
Instead a silent man's remote acclaim
An outpost, and a wind that nags and nags.

Millennium

Ah, some way there must be to end all this!
Ah, some way there must be to end all war!
Yes, there must be a way—and tiger jaws
Alike shall feel no need to feed more.

Souvenirs In The Meadow

Break not the crocus underneath
The soldier's boot of mire and clay.
The crocus is Love's souvenir
Of what was mine but yesterday.

Suppers Across The Sea

All the good things to eat that are far away
From the great dream of all my morale obtains;
What a tiger I'd be at the beef and the pork
Could I fight out this war with my knife and fork!

O'Donnell

"It's easy staying 'live—just use your head—"
Light words that young O'Donnell dryly said.
He knew, too, the grim and sorry rest
Of war, and died—just used his breast.

Dim By The Ditch

Through Monday's dark when we moved in to occupy our lines
The way led on past muddy sinks of bursted shell and mines
The ghastly mist there almost hid me from his boyish face
Half down the ditch, his head at drink, his dead arms still and slack.

*Pvt. Frederick de la Ronde submitted his first verse to The Stars and Stripes. At that time, he wrote: "These are the first of such verses that the war has brought out of me for better or worse. It is my hope to have a hundred or so of them published in the States under the title of 'Fours In Olive Drab' as they are quatrains, that is four lines to a verse, and the title derives from that and the fact they are quite plainly the verses of a man while carrying out his part of the war in olive drab." Shortly after having written this letter, De La Ronde was killed. Fulfilling his last request, we present his poems under the title he had chosen.

AWAKENING

The purple night has flown into the West,
And in the East young Phoebus starts anew
His journey, and the pearls of evening dew
Begin to vanish from the Earth's green breast;
In country ways the cock crows far and wide,
As from their sleep return the hosts of day,
Nocturnal creatures cease their work of play,
The chilly owl seeks his lair to hide;
Where darkness slept will come the shine
Of light on metal, and the voice of men,
To laugh and boast of petty deeds again,
Or start to seek more laughter and more wine
And rousing all, the Sergeant's thundrous shout:
"All right, youse lousy bums, I said 'Fall out.'"

—T-5 Harold P. Williams

POSTSCRIPT

Two things I'll miss this winter
As I shiver in my sack,
Are your cold feet implanted
In the middle of my back.
—S-Sgt. Gray Wilcox Jr.

LAMENT

I went for a Wac
With great velocity.
So sad: that lack
Of reciprocity.
—Tom Stack, Y1c

COME STA?

Felice is happy, *triste* is sad,
Buono is good and *cattivo* is bad;
Male is ill, *bene* is well,
Morto is dead and *war* is hell!
—Pvt. Clyde Hermann

FINALE

As can be told by any fule
During the joyous season of yule
You bring in the log, open the bottle,
There's no telling happen what'll.
—T-5 Hal Travis

TO A FATHERLESS BABE

The day he died,
His son was born.
Sweet sight denied,
Oh, hopeless morn
Such was to bring
To wife and boy
We now can't sing
Psalms of joy.

Dear orphaned lad,
You'll never know
Your worthy dad
Who sleeps below
The surging waves
With comrades true
In restless graves
So far from you.

Your mother's tears
Alas! will flow
Throughout the years.
It must be so.
And you will miss,
As you mature,
Your father's kiss,
His arm secure.

But, this believe:
I pray you will,
That we—too—grieve
For our pal, Bill.
And may his deeds
Help to imbue
All men and creeds
With love anew.

   —A. Blenderman, MAM 1-c

SNIPER IN FRANCE

The wonder of it stopped him where he was,
Stood him up straight and lean, and for a time
He lost the jungle prowl. The heavy slime
Of stealth unloosed his feet, the awful claws
Of fear released what they had stolen . . .
A little town of France was in bloom there,
Its cottages white-petaled. And the air
Carried in its arms the sun and scented pollen.

He was home. This was no foreign place—
He stood upon a little friendly street
In Pennsylvania, and it was sweet,
And loneliness made wet joy of his face,
The sniper's bullet struck him then. The pain
That instant made him animal again.

—Pvt. Donald J. Titus

OLD STONEWALL RIDES AGAIN

Midst shot and shell—a roarin' hell,
A vision gray astride;
Midst bursts and blood—a scarlet flood,
He reined in by my side.

"See hyeah, m'lad, have ye forgot,
"I, too, wuz trapp'd this way.
"Let 'for'ard' be your next command
"Till dusk descends today.

"The Shenando' wuz just like this;
"Forget your book and rule.
"Let's feint their front and reel their right;
"Retreat will win no duel.

"Then when the stars begin to sprout,
"We cross to yonder bank.
"At dawn they 'spect we hit from hyeah—
"Instead, we fire their flank.

All through the night—a lovely sight,
No clouds just cool and clear,
I watched her skies—her sparkling eyes
And Nature's silver sphere.

The whisperin' wind then told the trees
The news from neighbor's glen:
"Joe Yank is goin' to rout the Kraut,
" 'Cause 'Stonewall' rides again."

The eager trees then passed the word
Above our weary men:
"Joe Yank is goin' to rout the Kraut
" 'Cause 'Stonewall' rides again."

The news soon spread along the way
From field, up slope, down den:
"Joe Yank is going to rout the Kraut
" 'Cause 'Stonewall' rides again."

Old Sol began to stir and yawn,
His head, a golden glow,
As Jackson led our march to meet
The green-clad, block-head foe.

Our batteries a prelude roared
As Crutchfield led their fire,
Just like the days in Sixty-one
When Fremont was retired.

"Now 'on'ard' is our next command;
"Keep Kraut along his way.
"Yes, for'ard, don't check the pace
" 'Till dusk descends today."

A soft, sly smile began to creep
Across Ole "Stonewall's" face.
"*They run,*" he said; he drew his sword,
A slashing flash in chase.

We swept the fields and crossed the crests,
The Krauts, a scattered flock.
"Joe Yanks" we were, a generous troop—
We fed them lead and stock.

Midst shot and shell—a roarin' hell
Forget?—I'll never—when
Midst shout and rout—the routin' Krauts
Ole 'Stonewall' rides again.

—Robert Lawrence Henderson

NURSES -- CURSES

Sing us a song of pain and penance,
Army nurses are all lieutenants;
Whether they're blondes, brunettes or titians,
The hell of it is: they have commissions,
And privates, creatures of low degree,
Can dream, but never hope to be
More to the nurses who win their hearts
Than pulses, temperatures, graphs and charts.

—Pfc. C. C.

ON SEEING A DRUNKEN DOGFACE WITH A BUCK-TOOTHED GAL

When GIs get woozie
They ain't very choozy.

—Sgt. Leonard Summers

LIBERTY SHIP

Oh, gray steel ship with flag on high
Why must you always pass me by?
You brought me here, then went away
Am I forever doomed to stay
Upon these shores to which we sped?
You left me here and then you fled.
The name affixed to you is truly
One that was applied unduly—
For when we sailed across the sea
You ended then my Liberty!

—Lt. Roy Johnston

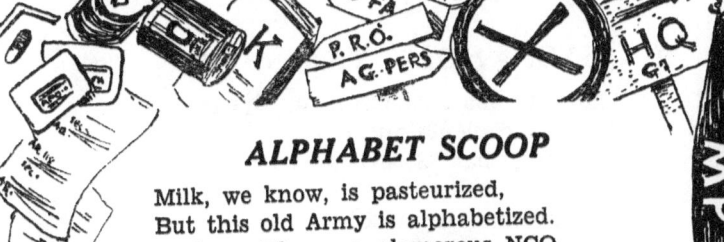

ALPHABET SCOOP

Milk, we know, is pasteurized,
But this old Army is alphabetized.
To be a Pfc. or a glamorous NCO,
You have to be authorized by a damn TO,
The CG in HQ and the BC in the CP
Throw ARs at a guy like me.
All is fubar, all is snafu, so—
The EM in the AAA at the APO
Get munched from the tough CO,
The SOS, the AGO, WOJG and CWO.
Whether it's AAF, QM, FA or FD,
The RA, AUS, NG, OCS or ERC,
The Army's not the place to be
If you never passed the ABC.
When you're on guard or on CQ,
Thinking is the only thing you do;
You remember the USO and the ARC,
And cuss the guys in the ASTP.
AWs are enforced by the OD,
VD is classified now as LD;
Even here across the seas,
We have trouble with the MPs.
Whether WAC, WAVE or GI,
No matter how hard you try—
This axiom is apparent yet,
The Army's run on the alphabet.

—Cpl. Norm Rachlin

STOCKHOLM TRAVELER

This war has nurtured many things,
Guns, and planes and tanks,
And, too, that "Stockholm Superman"
To whom we owe our thanks.
For superman he must be
To travel as he does,
One night he's in Berlin, and then
To Stockholm he will buzz.
He's called the "Stockholm Traveler,"
A fitting *nom de plume*,
He's very influential
For him there's always room
Aboard a plane that leaves Berlin,
Or Coblenz on the Rhine,
Wherever Allied bombs will fall
He'll be there, right on time.
He'll estimate the danger
To the city's power works,
He knows the weight of bombs that fell,
And the number out of work.
He knows that 46 percent
Of the water was destroyed,
And fifty heavy bombers crashed
From out that blackened void.
We're grateful to you, Traveler,
You keep us well supplied
With information that we want
Of the numbers that have died.
So Traveler with your info,
We find such little fault,
We can do naught but take it
With a good-sized grain of salt.

—Cpl. Joseph Quinn

REMARK ON THE CENSORED

I view with disdain,
This perennial rain,
For mine's the negative view,
Concerning permanent dew.
Our nocturnal floods
Are fine for the buds,
But sleep in a pool
I find rather cool.
Why stop to discuss it?
I'd much rather cuss it.
   —T-Sgt. Stan Swinton

R. I. P.

Here lies a Heinie
Cold and stiff,
He got no more
Than he tried to giff.

Here are the bones
Of Ludvig Von . . . sumpin',
He wasn't too good
At parachute jumpin'.

Wolfgang is gone
Alas and alack:
He never expected
To see such flak.

Fritz has returned
From whence he sprang;
Jolly good plane—
That Yank Mustang!
   —Pvt. David B. Wall

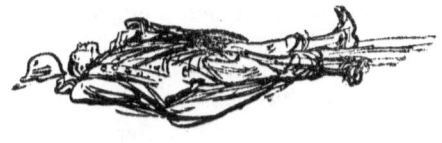

TITLE PAGE

He was a schoolmaster far from his books,
But he was in himself a kind of classroom;
He had the dignity of learned things;
There clung to him the fresh linen perfume
Of a new book . . . And his speech was
Purpled with strange pictorial words
That made his hearers eager children . . .
His eyes were hungry like a bird's—
He seemed always some beyond this time
And standing distant from this place;
His mind had a pursuant body—
Something of a young boy was his face . . .
He was a composition of his pupils,
He was a blackboard of a rare-like courage—
Death came to him as the next assignment:
The shell burst simply turned another page . . .

—Pvt. Donald J. Titus

VISITOR'S HOURS

A pair of soft brown eyes, now old with pain,
Looked into mine through tears like warm spring rain,
He whispered slowly, very haltingly,
"I'll be all right, they'll take good care of me."

I touched his fevered hand, smiled a bright smile.
"I'm sure you will, in just a little while."
And then in both our glances something died,
Because we each knew that the other lied.

—Pvt. R. Moore Smith, WAC

ROME

The grey-green tide, dried by the battle's heat,
No longer strong, is gone;
And white—starred mammoths, spewing dust,
Hesitate; then hurry north.
The guard has changed;
The seven hills still stand;
The lazy Tiber washes down to sea.
Father—(with God-given strength has watched
Armies march and die,
The glories that are cities fall in ruin.)
Victorious, transcendent, o'er the strife,
His Word and Work in an Eternal City linger on.
—Capt. I. I. Schulberg

PAX AMERICANA

Proud Rome whose cohorts ruled the world,
Thy Fabian swords are crumbled dust.
The legions' standards now are furled,
Ancient glory turned to dust.

Does Caesar sleep in restless grave,
Eager to rise and hasten forth,
With marching legions to smash this wave
Of Hun barbarians from the north?

Great Caesar, brave new armies stand
By Rubicon, where thy die was cast.
"Veni-vinci!" now our command,
Inspired by voices from the past.

And so in passing, time does repeat,
Your legions kept the Pax Romana.
In future years we vow to keep,
Nostri—Pax Americana.
—Pvt. Rob. Evans

HAPPY NEW YEAR

Blessings on thee, little man,
Barefoot boy, with cheeks of tan,
Better brush up on your Russian,
Learn to hate the dirty Prussian;
Take a course in airplane spotting
Also one for use in potting
Jerry, when above your airfields,
Back of walls or in the bare fields;
Learn to recognize Italians
Pasta, vino rossa, scallions.
Don't go near a booby trap,
Keep away from floating crap
Games, designed to part the rash
GI guy from all his cash;
Recognize the many ranks;
Learn the tricks of guns and tanks;
Appreciate we have no Merlin
Lore to lead us into Berlin,
That the fight goes to the fittest,
Not to him who dreams and sittest;
Learn all this, my child, and thee
Will know as much as forty-three.
—Sgt. H. E. George

COMPLAINT

The Puptent poems I have read
Give credence to the rumor
That fighters for the freedoms (four)
Are too devoid of humor.
—Pfc. Stewart Burke

THE LETTERS SOMEBODY DIDN'T WRITE

It ain't the heat nor the blistered feet,
Nor the meals of Spam in place of meat,
Nor the butter like lard, nor our turn at guard,
None of these is one-half as hard
As the jolt we get, after all the sweat,
And a cheery voice says, "No mail yet."

And it ain't the breeze, like a dragon's sneeze,
That peels the hide and weakens the knees,
Nor the dirt in your gun, nor the boiling sun—
These are forgotten when day is done,
But our voices fail and our faces pale
If we draw a blank when it's time for mail.

We can stand the flies and the sand in our eyes,
The orders, the rumors, the truths and the lies,
The mosquitoes' swarm and the water warm,
And the wards that reek of chloroform.
What takes our fight and makes throats tight
Are the letters somebody didn't write.

—Cpl. M. K. Lynds

NIX ON NASH

There appears to be a lamentable tendency in recent times
To imitate the unique and inimitable rhymes
Of Ogden Nash.
This trend is presumptuous and extremely rash
On the part of all parties concerned,
And all such contributions should be immediately burned
Or dropped quickly and quietly into File 13
(With the natural exception of this one, I mean.)

—S-Sgt Gray Wilcox, Jr.

ODE TO A GERMAN LANDSCAPE

Now, your trees stand leafless,
In desolate dignity against the sky.
Mute sentinels, keeping a somber watch
O'er the unmarked graves wherein
Your once so-vibrant bodies lie.
Oh, yes, my Aryan foe,
Our countryside still looks the same.
'Twas not so many ghastly months ago
That you and your unconquerable legions came,
In ordered, armored columns, row on row.
What say you now, rotting there,
You skulls, and bones, and sightless eyes?
Does not the ceaseless bray of Hitler's orat'ry,
His all too brutal butcheries of strife,
Shriek loudly to a blood red moon and sky:
"Only we are civilized . . ."

—Lt. H. J. Connor

HITLER'S ESCAPE

We are sorry they missed
As he should have been kissed
With a large hunk of steel in his head;
I think it's a shame
That it didn't have his name—
We'd be so doggoned pleased with him dead.
It tears hearts asunder
He's not six feet under
Making old Mother Earth his last bed.
(If you don't like this poem
Think up one of your own—
No one asked that the blamed thing be read!)
—Lt. Roy Johnston

AFTERTHOUGHT

Of woman fair the poet sings,
Of lips and hips and other things;
Of warm and winsome weaker sex,
Of models barefoot to their necks;
How sad that beauty so symmetrical
Should frequently become obstetrical.
—Sgt. H. E. George

WHISKY IS RISKY

I've seen today a GI poster
Of which we're urged to make the moster:
"Whisky is risky."
Straight talk, man to man—and sorely needed.
For who knows what rules of manly moderation might have gone unheeded
(And wild oats seeded)
As Christmas nears
(And gay New Years)—
Had we not known the truth
About this menace to our youth.
"Whisky is risky." Should we
Walk past that barrel house
On Corso Garibaldi
Ignoring scotch and rye
In fifths and quarts?
(It might cause warts!)
And nutty Bourbon?
(for fear of burpin'!)
Where is this whisky we must not risk?

—Cpl. W. S. Westcott

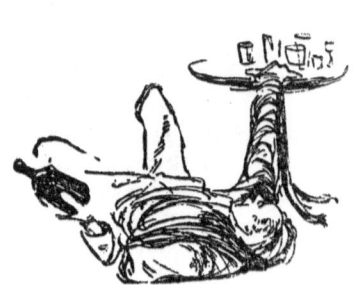

RUMOR

"They're either too young or too old" (so I hear),
"They're either too grey or too bright eyed and green.
"The pickings are poor is the word" (give a cheer!)
"And the girls in your wallet are safe and serene."
But after a letter containing this news
I find myself worried, uneasy and such:
If what the girls say is correct and quite true,
Then who in the hell do they marry so much?

—T-5 W. Feinberg

MY PISTOL, JEEP AND ME

I'm Technician Fifth Grade George P. Lahr
I'm easily espied,
You'll know me by my pistol
That keeps dangling from my side.
I tie one string around my thigh
And let one hang on down,
You can tell when I have passed you
By the trail that's on the groun'.
My job is very easy, but by now it's getting stale,
Day by day the same routine, I'm picking up the mail.
I start in dark and early, no time for rest or sleep,
I grab me trusty forty-five and hop into my jeep.
I average 50 on the road
And 60 through the town,
But when I spot an MP
I bring it slightly down.
I visit every APO
From Gela to Paterno
And when I pass I grab a glass
And shoot the old *buon giorno*.
I like to go out on the road
And travel wide and far
And bump into some guys I know
Who call me Sergeant Lahr.
I make my friends or enemies
As they get mail or miss,
There's guys that get their daily batch
While some blame me and hiss.
Hooray for me! To hell with the men!
They never believe I've tried,
So I'm left to shake the hand that shook
The pistol on my side.
It seems to me I should rate more
For my effort and devotion.
I hope I get those sergeant's stripes
The next list of promotion.
—T-5 George P. Lahr
Sept. 10, 1943

PUPTENT PROMOTION

My name is Technician Fourth Grade George P. Lahr,
You'll never hear me gripe,
Since writing a poem for your paper
I got me extra stripe.
—T-4 George P. Lahr
Sept. 14, 1943

HELLO KID

"Hello kid, glad to see you,
Did you make that fight for Rome?
Did you stand on Alban hillsides
And spot St. Peter's Dome?

"Were you tanned by scorching sunshine,
Were you drenched by chilling rain,
Were you hungry, sore and blistered,
As you fought for every gain?

"Did you get your share of vino
With each little town you took?
Bet you swiped some chickens, too
Say, who in hell was cook?

"Did the Pizons yell and cheer you
As your column came in view?
Did you praise the little Piper cub
That high above you flew?

"Did you ask the Man in Heaven
To blacken out the sun,
So that darkness would protect you
From the searching eyes of Hun?

"When you broke out of the mountains
And you rode through Roman streets,
Did you get a little homesick
By the way a Roman greets?

"Did you brush up on Italian
With the famous 'Veni qua,'
And learn to pass the time of day
With Pizon come sta?

"Did your thoughts go back to Jersey
Or wherever you might dwell?
Did this seem just like a heaven
After coming out of hell?

"Well, sure was nice to meet you, chum—
Mighty glad I did—
You gotta go, well best of luck—
And take it easy, kid—."
—T-Sgt. T. J. Dorman

THE HOME SCENE

It isn't that she's true to me,
There's just no opportunity,
To let a 4-F make a pass . . .
Thank Heaven, they have rationed gas!
—T-Sgt. Stan Swinton

POULTRY

At sweet sixteen I first began
To ask you, Santa, for a girl;
At seventeen, you will recall
I wanted someone strong and small.
The Christmas that I reached eighteen,
I fancied someone sweet—my dream.
And at nineteen, I was quite sure
I'd fall for someone more mature.
At twenty, I still thought I'd find
Romance in someone with a Mind.
I retrogressed at twenty-one
And found the farmer's girl more fun.
My viewpoint changed at twenty-two,
I longed for someone who'd be true.
I broke my heart at twenty-three,
And asked for any girl, if kind to me.
Then begged at blissful twenty-four
For anyone who wouldn't bore.
Now, Santa, that I'm twenty-five,
Please send me any girl alive.
—Pvt. George Dzurich

ANY QUESTIONS

ROME, bah!
Home . . . ah!
—Pvt. Ben Dinkowski

VERIFIED

The letter which I wrote recalled to mind
Many pleasant memories, laughing days
When we were young. "Why, he's on the line!"
A friend replied, when I was searching ways
To forge again the link of our spirit's chain
The letter which I wrote raced Time. I meant to cheer
You, raise your spirits high, laugh once again
At people, places, things and Life—at Death, near
Each road's bending: it would have helped, I know.
With it went my heart, my love, my prayer
To guide you through the battle, my way to show
I had not forgotten. Today, my letter returned from where
You met your Maker—God knows you tried
For stamped across your name: "Returned to Sender—Verified."
—F. O. Doug Wallace

MINES

Of all the combat units,
It had to fall our lot
To pick up mines, safety them,
Directly on the spot.
With 50 yards of half-inch rope.
We carefully made a lap,
Or stepped down a rocky slope
To pull a booby-trap,
So men, learn your lesson well,
It's better for your breath:
For any time you spot a mine,
You're shaking hands with Death.
—Pfc. D. James Sawyer

WE ASK BUT THIS

We know that many questions will arise
Within your mind ... questions to ask
Of desolate islands and of shell-torn skies,
Of blood ... and filth ... and death ... of swarming flies;
Of weary duty through the night ... of torturing tasks
Which scourge the living as a comrade dies.

We know that you will ask the temporal thrill
Of tales born from the womb of mute despair ...
A graphic picture of the human lust to kill,
Of swamps, gut-deep in mud ... of cratered hill
We took by hell's own punishment ... the echoing blare
Of bugle, and the "forward march" while time stood still.

But when we come again ... we who come home
From out this world-inferno, souls seared deep;
Ask not of us, for grandizement, a written tome
To cherish as historic lore, with froth and foam ...
Just let us rest awhile within the deep
And pregnant silence, never more to roam.

Give us clean sheets, and blue cups brimming-filled;
Give us gay laughter flowing over tears;
Give us forgetfulness of things which thrilled
You in your reading ... Let tired hearts be stilled
To gentle silence through the fruitful years
Which needs must come ... warmth for hearts long chilled.

Just give us this. Is this too much to say,
We who have prayed, through hell and back, for such a day?

—Sgt. Will D. Muse

POSTLUDE

What happens when the bugles cease to spill
Their early morning song across the hill?
And once-clean guns are laid aside to rust—
And once-strong men are crumbling piles of dust?

What happens when the tattered banners fall
Defeated—and the final battle call
Has died away across the distant fields,
And friend and foe alike lay down their shields?

What happens when the treaty inks are dry
And men refuse to kill—refuse to die?
When battle-wearied men go home again—
Tell me warrior, what happens then?

—Pfc. Maynard Johnson

FINAL DUTY

And when, at last, there will be none to come
Against us, brandishing the lordly saber,
And when plunder of that sword shall be reclaimed
And peace be on the earth, shall not our labor
Be unfinished until the beast be tamed
Within us, and we walk the living loam
Of motherland, and find again our neighbor,
And build an honest house and call it home?

—T-4 Max V. Exner

PROSPECT

And in the days to come,
Unbelievably distant still,
Someone is sure to ask—
What was it like?
And I shall stare at him
Vacant of eye
Sluggish to catch the meaning of his question
But in my heart, the past will rip apart
Indignant gashes; fear will bleed again
My hand will move
To brush aside the madness
Recalled to consciousness.
My lips will close
In bitter line upon the caustic word
And all of me will turn the overtones
Of curious watching into frozen shame—
The pent up silence of a zero hour.

—Pfc. Hans Juergensen-Steinhart

TIME OUT OF MIND

I'm weary of this breathing
In a brain-suspended state.
I'm surfeited with living
Where there is no present date.
I've dwelt too long in memories
Of happy yesterday;
I've held too much of dreaming
Of tomorrow's bright array.
But, there are naught but yesterdays
And naught but sweet tomorrows
To feed the starving heart on
In this world of hate and sorrow.
I pray that Fate will speed the hour,
When Peace will mark its sway
So I may sail for home's far shores,
And the land of full todays!

—Lt. John T. Weaver

WHAT IS WAR

What is war? Some day your child may ask:
What is war? A question indeed to force you to turn from your appointed task.
Well, I'll tell you now and you may well remember
So you can answer if asked in June or December.
War is battle, blood and toil
War is death on a foreign soil
War is business, production in bloom
War is a wife, who, wanting to be near her husband, eats, sleeps and bathes in one room.
War is overtime pay, swing shifts and strikes
War is rationing, air-raid drill and no tires for bikes.
War is a cause for a lot of new slants,
War makes women taxi-drivers, welders, carpenters, plumbers and miners, and they still don't look good in pants
War is bonds, contributions, and taxes,
War is meant to beat the Axis
War was described by a man named Sherman
War is a billion dollar enterprise, giving millions of people employment, destroying countries for centuries so we can kill a Jap or a German.
The best thing about war is akin to hitting yourself on the head with a hammer, right on the top.
It feels so good when we stop.

—T-Sgt. Ralph B. Steiner

MANIFESTO

What lasting peace can now be gained
With nations rotten to their core?
What foolish words of peace remain
To haunt our minds forevermore?
Be gone—and die, each one of you
Who thinks the world is his to rule.
Awake, awake, you men in whom
We did entrust our nation's bloom.
We want a peace—a peace our own
With no more fears of carnage wrought;
We want to live a life full grown—
It must be so—this peace when bought.

—Sgt. William Tully

UKASE

When this is over
And we come home again,
Forget the band
And the cheers from the stand;
Just have the things
Well in hand—
The things we fought for.
Understand?
                —Pfc. C. G. Tiggas

TO REVOLUTIONISTS

Let my only contribution
To a future revolution
Be a smile;
And instead of making battle
Let me wield a fool's red rattle,
Without guile.
For I've noted that dictators
Leave me short of meat and 'taters
Every time
They start calling for damnation
Of the thinkers of their nation,
(What's my rhyme?)
And that wars don't spring from laughter
Nor are fat men fond of slaughter,
(What a word!)
But that those who love to chuckle
Are reluctant more to buckle
On the sword,
So when rabble-rousers riot,
And disturb my peace and quiet
For a while,
And fanatics come a-pushin'
Me to join their revolution,
I shall smile.
                —Capt. F. T. Grant

WHEN I RETURN

When I return,
I want no blare of trumpets,
Cheering, shouting noise;
I want no wild acclaim,
People shrieking madly—
"Hats off, here come our boys!"

When I return,
Just make it quiet
And calmly grip my hand.
Look into my eyes once more—
I'll understand.
Then let me see the beauty of homes,
Trees and the valleys,
Places I once knew,
The things we once took for granted,
'Til war hid them from view.

I want no blare of trumpets,
Cheering, shouting . . . noise.
Just let me see you smile—
Forgotten is the war.
Dearest, even now I need these things,
When I return, much more.
—T-Sgt. J. D. Rovick

HOME FROM WAR

Who can say at war's end
"We are lucky living men?"
After so much of us has died
How can we be satisfied
That we, the so-called living men,
Will find a way to live again?
For when a man has daily faced
The brute within him, low, debased,
Can he look forward to the light,
Wipe out the memories of the fight
Forget the strange erotic bliss
That comes with some cheap purchased kiss?
Ah, no! And it will be his fateful lot
To live on and find that he lives not
Though like the living we'll behave
We'll be the dead without a grave.
—Cpl. Anthony Carlin

HOMECOMING

I hope I'll be home again
When autumn kisses summer green
And turns it soft and brown
Like your hair in the lamplight
Of a quiet evening:
To see again the winter mantle
Turn the city white and clean
And watch the kids go belly whopping
Down the big hill in the park,
To feel again my feet in civvy shoes
Slap the clean, hard asphalt
Of the city streets
While we're window shopping for furniture;
To see you again
Across the table in the morning;
To know again
The taste of life warm and rich;
And soft arms
And a bosom to take my troubles to
When I want to be a little boy again.

—Pfc. Harry Olive

FAULTS

When I come back if I should swear
A little now and then,
Remember—
I have lived with men
Who thought it manly
Swearing . . .X; XXXX!
If I should get a beautiful snootful
Of good American drink
Remember—
I have drunk some stuff
They'd mix with paint at home—
I craved a decent drink!
When I come back 'twill take
A little while to learn to live
A sane civilian life again . . .
So for a month or so I'll just acclimatize
Myself and lose those faults
I may have gained,
Or have not lost as yet.

—Lt. John V. Peterson

POSTWAR WORRIES

You may have thought the change quite rough
From civilian to GI,
But in reverse
T'will be much worse,
And here are reasons why:

Coming home was really grand
War was something of the past;
The hometown cheered
While trumpets blared
And the man's heart beat fast.

But Mom's pride was deeply hurt
When you ignored her silverware,
Her linen white,
And china bright—
For you preferred your old mess gear.

And brother Johnny stared in wonder
When you pulled covers from the bed,
Let out a snore
Upon the floor,
And slept like someone dead.

And when Sis came in for morning shower,
She thought it most amazing
You sitting there
On linoleum bare
With steel helmet, shaving.

But finale came when neighbors gasped,
'Twas a sight they'd never seen.
You dug a hole,
Quite in Army role
And used it for a latrine.
          —Pvt. H. Hollingsworth

VETERANS' AID

So many things they've promised us
Our burdens will be carried,
And like wide eyed kids at Christmas time
Our wants are great and varied.

Some want a farm with many cows,
While others will acknowledge
They want a job, a happy home
Or chance to go to college.

Despite the many promises
There's one thing I would take
Don't give me special privileges—
Give me just an even break.

—Pvt. William Hudson

THE CALL--A CRY OR SONG?

After I have learned to face the foe
And mastered all the rules of war,
How shall I answer the call to peace?
How shall I live the life I knew before?
In former days of peace I also fought,
In daily frays of wrong and right;
The foe had rules I did not know,
And I had none to guide me in the fight.
I fear the call to peace that comes in song,
When men will raise their hearts in joy,
And cast their eyes towards tranquil homes,
The lodestone of the soldier boy.
Let the call to peace be clear this time,
No choir singing—"Buddy, can you, spare a dime?

—Pfc. Marshall Keller

NO SPLENDOR HERE

So this is war, no splendor here.
No martial music, no crowds to cheer
Nothing but harsh reality
Of the price we must pay for victory.
For the lads of Cassino and Anzio
These thoughts are worthless; too well you know
Of the terrible misery and biting cold
Endured at the front in a muddy hole
Of Italy's mountains and Africa's sand,
Of night patrols in no man's land;
Of nobler comrades and nobler dead
Who battled on till the snow turned red.
Even the glorious heaven above
God's perfect promise of peace and love
Is desecrated by roaring plane
Out on a mission of death and pain.
Oh, God, how long are we to stand
Man's inhumanity to man?

—Pfc. Cecil V. Groseclose

TITLE INDEX

A

ABOUT AN ABBEY	14
AFTERTHOUGHT	97
AH, SWEET MYSTERY	23
AH, WILDERNESS	16
AIR RAID	19
ALIBI	32
ALPHABET SCOOP	89
AMBITION	44
AND NOW, OCTOBER	59
AND THEN	78
ANY QUESTIONS	102
ANZIO	15
ARC DANCE	44
ARE YOU NERVOUS IN THE SERVICE?	74
ASSURANCE	28
ATLANTIC CHARTER	59
AWAKENING	82

B

BASIC ENGLISH	12
BATTLE	18
BEACH PARTY	39
BEN AHMED	22
BEYOND ALL POWER	78
BUMPS	64

C

CALL, THE	112
CHANGE	68
CHRISTMAS EVERY DAY	62
COME STA?	83
COMING CLEAN	74
COMPARISON	34
COMPLAINT	94
CONVERSATION WITH A MULE	24
CO's PRAYER, THE	38
CORONA CAMPAIGN, THE	75
CORPORAL PETTIFER'S PEACE	42
COTE D'OR	39
COURTSHIP IN ITALY	16
CROSSING	7

D

DANTE AND BEATRICE, TO	58
D-DAY INTROSPECTION	38
DESIRE	79

DIARY OF A NURSE	49
DIRTY GERTIE	4
DJEBEL AKROUTA	8
DOUBTFUL COMFORT	33
DRUNKEN DOGFACE	88

E

EL GUETTAR	8
ENCORE	12
ENIGMA	56
EVEN THEN	29

F

FANNY OF TRAPANI	4
FAULTS	110
FIELD MOVIE	2
FINAL DUTY	105
FINALE	83
FIRST LOVE	53
FORBIDDEN DRINK	64
FOURS IN OLIVE DRAB	80
FRANC, THE	23

G

GENERAL McNAIR AND SON, TO	68
GI LOVE LETTER	67
GI PROFILES	52
GOUM	55
GREENHORNS	52
GRIPE POEM	56

H

HANDS	2
HAPPY BIRTHDAY, BUD	72
HAPPY NEW YEAR	94
HAPPY SOLDIERS	73
HATRED'S YIELD	1
HELLO KID	100
HEY BUD	3
HOME FROM WAR	109
HOME SCENE, THE	102
HOME TO A HOSS	72
HOMECOMING	110
HITLER'S ESCAPE	97

I

I HUNT TODAY	19
I WONDER	49
IMPEDIMENTA	13
IN CAROLINE	63
IN CONSTANTINE	9
IN MEMORIAM	33

J

JAUNDICE IS JAUNTY	35

K

KEEPSAKE	58
KILLER'S VALENTINE	33

L

LAMENT	83
LAW IN MY HANDS	54
LET ME	53
LETTER TO AMERICA	51
LETTERS SOMEBODY DIDN'T WRITE, THE	95
LIBERTY SHIP	88
LITERARY CRITICISM	17
LITTLE BANKROLL	65
LITTLE THINGS	79
LOGIC	64
LUSCIOUS LENA	5

M

MADNESS	7
MANIFESTO	107
MARIE OF NAPOLI	5
MINE LAYERS	37
MINES	103
MISSING IN ACTION	54
MONEY'S FUNNY	22
MULE REPLIES, THE	25
MY NAME IS TINA	6
MY PISTOL, JEEP AND ME	99

N

NEWS, THE	61
NIGHT CAPPED	73
NIGHT RAID	41
NIX ON NASH	95
NO BED OF ROSES	16
NO SPLENDOR HERE	113
NON-COMBATANT	40
NOT IF, BUT WHEN	46
NOT IN BROOKLYN	50
NURSES—CURSES	88

O

OBLIVION	66
OBSERVATION	49
ODE OF LAMENT	12
ODE TO A GERMAN LANDSCAPE	96
OLD STONEWALL RIDES AGAIN	86

OLIVE TREES	36
ONE TALENT	46
ORDER	3

P

PASSIONATE COMPANY CLERK, THE	27
PAX AMERICANA	93
PEOPLE SPEAK, THE	72
POSTLUDE	105
POSTSCRIPT	83
POSTWAR WORRIES	111
POTENT ABDULLAH	9
POULTRY	102
PROSPECT	106
PUPTENT PROMOTION	99

R

RAIN-SOAKED	22
RANGERS, THE	20
REMARK ON THE CENSORED	91
REMEMBER, DEAR	32
REQUEST	67
RESPECTFULLY SUGGESTED	49
RESPITE	48
REVERIE	77
R.I.P.	91
RIPONE DEL VAST	11
ROME	93
RUMOR	98

S

SCHOOLDAY SWEETHEART	30
SEASON'S GREETINGS	62
SITUATION NORMAL	26
SITUATION STILL NORMAL	26
SKY PATHS	40
SNIPER IN FRANCE	85
SOLDIERS IN A CAFE	30
SOLITAIRE	53
SONGSTERS SING	41
STOCKHOLM TRAVELER	90
SUPPLY	50
SUPPOSING	32

T

TANK MEN	60
TASTE THE NIGHTBANE	29
TELL ME, POP	70
TEMPUS FUGIT	2
THOUGHT	66
THREE CHEERS FOR THE APO	71

TIME OUT OF MIND	106
TIMID WOLF	56
TITLE PAGE	92
TO A CIVILIAN INSECT	45
TO A FATHERLESS BABE	84
TO A MESSKIT	13
TO HIDE A LOVE	28
TO REVOLUTIONISTS	108
TO SALERNO	14
TO THE MASTER RACE	69
TREMENDOUS WINGS	10
TRIBUTE	55
TRILOGY	47
TRUCK DRIVERS	65
TWINKLE, TWINKLE	65

U

UKASE	108
UNENDING TIME	47
UNPRINTABLE THOUGHT	70
UNREQUITING	13

V

V-MAIL MABEL	45
VERIFIED	103
VERONA	61
VETERANS' AID	112
VISITOR'S HOURS	92
VON ARNIM'S LAST STAND	31

W

WAR MAKES MEN, THE	50
WAR SUMMARY	48
WAR WIDOW	73
WEAKER SEX, THE	71
WE ASK BUT THIS	104
WE WON'T FORGET	36
WHAT IS WAR	107
WHEN I RETURN	109
WHEN DUTY CALLED	76
WHISKEY IS RISKY	98
WINGLESS VICTORY	55
WITH UNDYING LOVE	18
WOUNDED	39
WRITTEN AT THE GRAVES OF KEATS AND SHELLEY	57

Y

YOU ARE MORALE	69
YOU WILL BE OLD	10

INDEX TO AUTHORS

Name	Page
A	
Anderson, William A.	79
Allchin, Floyd	5
Ammons, James D.	63
Arnold, Bud	72
B	
Barrett, Edwin J.	61
Bendityky, Eddie	74
Betonti, A. J.	26
Bivona, Francesco	59
Blenderman, A.	84
Botten, E. W.	50
Branch, Leroy C.	33
Brandels, Hal	23
Brown, Russell	77
Brundle, Frederick	6
Burke, Robert B.	14
Burke, Stewart	94
C	
Callahan, William	67
Campbell, Liberty	55
Campbell, Paul R.	48
Carlin, Anthony	33, 109
Carroll, C. W., Jr.	67
Chernick, Hank	26
Church, Jimmie	55
Coatell, Walter	45
Cobb, Chad	73
Cochran, Winifred	10
Cohen, Larry	71
Colker, Shirley	18
Colling, J. M.	36
Colosacco, E. H.	13
Conner, F. D.	4
Connor, H. J.	96
Cooper, Owen	65
Countess, J. D.	18
Craig, Rose C.	22, 49, 52
Critton, J. H.	75
D	
Dallaire, Victor	22
Davenport, H. S.	13
David, Samuel I.	30
Decker-Boyle, M. A.	9
Dewey, Robert J.	36
De la Ronde, Frederick	80
De Munbrun, Roland	41
De Reimer, Lewis P.	66
Diener, David E.	49
DiGiorgio, John	28, 53
Dinkowski, Ben	102
Dorman, T. J.	100
Dower, Dorothy E.	48
Downey, Fairfax	74
Dunne, James F.	5
Dzurich, George	102
E	
Edwards, Gene D. W.	35
Emley, Charles E.	40
Evans, Rob	93
Evel, Tom	47
Exner, Max V.	105
F	
Feinberg, W.	98
Fischer, Fred	5
Foner, Henry J.	2, 27
G	
Galowitz, Edward	72
George, H. E.	94, 97
Gibson, Stanley R.	11
Goldberg, Leon W.	68
Goodrich, James I.	73
Goodwin, Hooker	30
Grant, Fulton T.	38, 42, 43, 108
Greenberg, Max	56
Groseclose, Cecil V.	113
Gumm, Jay	16

Name	Page	Name	Page
H			
Haakenson, Bob	50	Hobb, Ben	40, 46
Henderson, Robert L.	86	Hoff, Edwin J.	39
Hermann, Clyde	83	Hollingsworth, H.	111
Hiorns, Richard	24	Hudson, William	112
I			
Irwin, Wallace, Jr.	31		
J			
Jasowitz, Edward	16	Johnston, Roy	88, 97
Jeck, Randolph	12	Juergensen-Steinhart, Hans	29, 106
Johnson, Manyard	105		
K			
Keller, Marshall	112	Knighten, Bernard	25
Kenyner, Robert D.	12	Kravchick, S.	32
Keyes, William L.	32	Krutchik, Phil	44
L			
Lahr, George P.	99	Levy, N. N.	17
Lehman, Milton	51	Lovett, R. W.	62, 64
Levins, Sue	28	Lynds, M. K.	95
M			
Mackey, Henry B.	50	Mercer, M. E.	9
Masque, Sgt.	3	Modica, Robert	32
McCoy, George	16	Muse, Will D.	104
N			
Nantell, John P.	1, 56	Newton, Tom	13
Newcomb, R. R.	8		
O			
Olive, Harry	2, 53, 110	Oulahan, Richard, Jr.	15
P			
Peterson, Harold S.	53	Popperwell, Stanley	14
Peterson, John V.	41, 45, 110		
Q			
Quinn, Joseph	90		
R			
Rachlin, Norm	89	Reese, Louis, Jr.	69
Radosta, John	49	Reynolds, Ray	7
Rainear, Chick	61	Riley, F.	20, 21
Rantanen, Irving E.	57	Ritter, Max	68

Name	Page	Name	Page
Rivlin, Ben D.	44	Rubright, R. W.	34
Robichaud, Frank	52	Russell, William L.	4
Rovick, J. D.	109	Rust, Ed	64

S

Name	Page	Name	Page
Sampas, S. G.	29, 39	Shershow, Harry	72
Sawyer, D. James	12, 78, 103	Shuman, Samuel B.	33
Sayers, E. G.	22	Smith, R. Moore	92
Schneider, A.	19	Stack, Tom	83
Schulberg, I. I.	93	Stebbing, F. J.	46
Scott, Virgil	2, 59, 79	Steiner, Ralph B.	107
Shaw, Marvin	54	Summers, Leonard	88
Sheehan, John L.	10	Swinton, Stan	91, 102
Shenfield, Lawrence W.	66	Sybert, G. G.	65

T

Name	Page	Name	Page
Tausend, Milton E.	39, 60	Titus, Donald J.	58, 85, 92
Thompson, E. H.	38	Travis, Hal	83
Tiggas, C. G.	108	Tully, William	107

V

Name	Page	Name	Page
Vezmar, S.	47	Volk, Harry P.	73
Viereck, Peter	37		

W

Name	Page	Name	Page
Wall, David B.	91	Westcott, W. S.	62, 98
Wallace, Doug	54, 55, 58, 69, 103	Westerberg, Carl D.	3
Weaver, John T.	19, 56, 106	Wheaton, Ray	8
Weil, Bill	64	Wilcox, Gray, Jr.	49, 71, 83, 95
Weil, Lester	7	Williams, Harold P.	82
Weinstein, S.	70	Willig, John	23
West, O. D.	78	Wronker, Bob	65, 70

www.ingramcontent.com/pod-product-compliance
Lightning Source LLC
Chambersburg PA
CBHW030142170426
43199CB00008B/169